HOMOSEXUALITY:
A SYMBOLIC CONFUSION

Ruth Tiffany Barnhouse

A Crossroad Book

THE SEABURY PRESS · NEW YORK

1977
The Seabury Press
815 Second Avenue
New York, N.Y. 10017

Printed in the United States of America

Library of Congress Cataloging in Publication Data

Barnhouse, Ruth Tiffany, 1923–
Homosexuality: a symbolic confusion.
"A Crossroad book."
Includes bibliographical references.
1. Homosexuality. I. Title.
RC558.B36   155.3   76–52749   ISBN 0–8164–0303–1

CONTENTS

PART III

Problems in Transition from "What Is" to "What Ought To Be"

PART IV

"What Ought To Be"—Some Theological Reflections

To my children,
Pete, Ruth, Bob, Will, Chris, Tom and John

Foreword

Once upon a time there were men and women who liked being men and women. They particularly enjoyed the sense of otherness that the constant reminder of the fact of *two* sexes gave them. But there were others who did not like that particular fact. They preferred their own sex to the other sex and found their otherness in rejecting otherness. For a long time they kept quiet about their feelings, though it was clear to many who watched them and listened to them that they were what they were. Some of the two-sex party found entertaining the efforts of the one-sex adherents to encompass all sexual activity within one-sex. Some found it disagreeable, so unpleasant in fact that they caused laws to be passed against it. But as with all things against which laws are passed, it developed a large number of supporters. Furthermore, there were countless occasions and environments in which only one sex was to be found. This helped to swell the numbers of practitioners and supporters of monosexuality. Gradually the monosexualists discovered their power. They created a monosexual esthetic, a monosexual ethic, and finally, in a world in which everything had been politicized, a monosexual politics. They had arrived. They were a political force, a talking, marching, propagandizing minority that demanded to be listened to and understood and dealt with exactly as racial and ethnic minorities insisted on being heard and acknowledged. They achieved much of what they sought, almost everything except that form of quota hiring and quota representation that in the late twentieth century took on the name of "affirmative action." As for the men and women who had liked being men and women, especially in a two-sex world, a fair number of them were not always so sure now about their sexual selves. On certain occasions, in certain environments, they wondered if they were the minority and should begin to organize, to march, to demand *their* rights.

We have all lived through this legend of lost-and-found sexuality. History has lived through it several times. But only in our time has homosexual propaganda achieved such proportions and the appeal against the sadistic mistreatment of homosexuals developed such sympathy that homosexuality needs to be examined at such length, with such care, with such understanding. It can no longer be dealt with in the terms of a single discipline. While it can be usefully examined within the competencies of psychoanalysts and psychiatrists, sociologists and anthropologists, philosophers and historians, it has, rightly or wrongly, made such large-scale claims and occupied sugh a significant place in a society fixated on smashing all closet doors and exposing all privacies, that we can no longer postpone that searching speculation about human performance that only a value-centered mind can bring to the subject of homosexuality. That is what Ruth Tiffany Barnhouse has done in this book. The result is not only an extraordinarily responsible and engaging work, but a sharp focusing on what the destruction of privacy had all but carried away with it, an attention to underlying values.

There is no question in my mind that Dr. Barnhouse, speaking as psychiatrist and theologian, is right in insisting that final judgments on matters of the consequence of homosexuality are made on the basis of a society's underlying values. As she says at the end of Chapter Four, "No matter how solid the scientific evidence may be for the presence or absence of pathology, it will ultimately be up to society to decide whether or not, or under what conditions, homosexual behavior will be tolerated." Ruth Barnhouse is a tough-minded professional in the world of the psyche and she sees accurately and in detail where and how sexual behavior finds its strengths and weaknesses, its sanctions, oppressions, and freeings. But she is also that rarest of religious thinkers, one who theologizes rather than moralizes. The effect of this is not to dislodge our sense of sin, but rather to take it entirely away from shallow categories of acceptance or dismissal and into that value-centered world of freedom in which a personel ego can grow and be nourished by otherness and its tensions and conflicts.

This is a nourishing book, a nurturing one. It moves with clarity and grace from the general to the special, from *what is*, to use the author's terms, to *what ought to be.* It deals even-handedly with conflagration issues, such as the American Psychiatric Association's change of diagnostic classification of homosexuality from deviation to simply "one form of sexual behavior," or the various arguments and exhortations for the normality or neutrality of homosexuality. It makes clear, beyond controversy, the case for decriminalization of homosexuality. And just as unmistakably, it sets forth the case for an adult sexuality against which the incompleteness of homosexuality can only be seen as a stunted sexuality. The argument that the homosexual life is the result of unconscious conditioning is answered with classical precision, for even in the realm of the unconscious we make choices for which we are responsible: "As adults, we are constituted by all that has happened to us, and by all our responses to the sum of these internal and external events."

Should homosexuals, then, turn away from this book? Will they feel themselves dismissed by it? On the contrary, they must read it, I think, because they are so warmly met in it, so thoughtfully discussed, so gracefully gathered into a narrative in which everyone's sexuality is at issue.

Barry Ulanov

Introduction

*I*n a scholarly and profound article which deals with some of the issues raised in contemporary society by the lively interest and extensive research in human sexuality, Dr. Robert Stoller has written that "we may not solve these moral questions, which masquerade as scientific ones, as easily as either side hopes." It is this dual aspect of the problem of homosexuality that I have chosen to address. To those of my readers who have studied for the ministry or priesthood, it will not seem strange that I have written here both as a psychiatrist and as a theologian. In the course of their education, members of the clergy have to learn a great deal about human psychology; many work in mental health facilities, at least for a time. The training of psychiatrists and psychologists tends to be more one-sided: nobody requires them to take a course which will tell them when, in the best interests of their patients, it would be wise to secure the services of the clergy. Although a recent survey conducted by the American Psychiatric Association discloses that formal affiliation with a church or temple is statistically higher for psychiatrists than for the general population, my experience suggests to me that many psychiatrists must keep their religion and their science rigidly separated from one another. I hope that those among them who read this book may decide that a mingling of the two ways of looking at the care of souls can be more fruitful than they realized.

In Part I, I expose the ongoing tension between science and theology and indicate what I think is the appropriate domain of each discipline and how each might usefully cooperate with the other. Part II reviews the information about homosexuality which is currently available through the various scientific disciplines which have been applied to it. Part III raises the contemporary ethical questions which I feel have received insufficient formal attention, and which proceed directly out of the scientific findings. In Part IV I begin the task of addressing those questions theologically. I believe that sex is one of the central symbols of religion which has been both misinterpreted and neglected through much of Christian history. This theological failure has contributed to the persistence of various forms of the dualist heresies in both their secular and religious forms; extreme asceticism and materialism are obvious examples. This misinterpretation and neglect has also contributed to the continuing warfare between mysticism and rationality. These are not, as many theologians and nearly all scientists have supposed, incompatible ways of experiencing the world; on the contrary, I would go so far as to say that the understanding of *any* phenomenon, be it interior or exterior, material or immaterial, of any nature whatsoever, is seriously distorted and limited unless its study is approached both mystically *and* rationally. I regret the limitations of time and space which forced the condensation of the material in support of this view into two chapters and the omission of much that is relevant. My debt to Carl Jung, Teilhard de Chardin, Owen Barfield, Charles Davis, and many others will be obvious in this section. Less obvious, but at least as important, is my debt to the modern interpretation of the Spiritual Exercises of St. Ignatius of Loyola, as I had the good fortune to learn something of them at Weston School of Theology, most particularly from my own director, Father Robert Doherty, S. J.

Work which eventually led to the writing of this book began several years ago when I was first asked to lecture on homosexuality at Weston School of Theology in Cambridge, Massachusetts. It was in response to those lectures that I received the first help which requires grateful acknowledgement: the students asked many questions which I never would have thought of at that time and the exhilarating discussions which followed—discussions with Jesuits are always exhilarating—opened up many new lines of inquiry, both scientific and theological.

Throughout the book I have avoided, often after considerable stylistic struggle, the use of "sexist" language. Only occasionally have I used the word *man* in its generic sense, but where it is so used I have capitalized it. The few such references are not complimentary so I hope that my linguistically militant sisters will not be seriously offended. Perhaps they may react as did the young girl I know who, in the course of a parlor game involving the frequently hilarious substitution of *person* for *man* in as many terms as we could imagine, said, when it came to Portuguese-person-of-war: "You know, there are some things I would just as soon let them have!" Vigilant readers will perhaps spot the few places where *they* has been used generically after a single noun instead of *he,* which we have all been taught is the only correct usage. I am indebted to Rosa Shand Turner for bringing to my attention the fact that this use of *he* is a recent invention of androcentric grammarians, mostly on this side of the Atlantic, and that according to the *Oxford English Dictionary, they* is perfectly acceptable.

For editorial skill in organizing the astonishingly discursive transcripts of the tapes of the original lectures at Weston, I am most grateful to Elizabeth Eidlitz. My efficient and enthusiastic research assistants at various stages of the project were Cheri Stevenson, Margaret Murdoch Ladd, Elizabeth Kreilkamp, and Phyllis Leith. I am particularly grateful to Virginia Hall, without whose expert secretarial and research services, including the cataloging of my library, the work would hardly have been possible. Also invaluable and appreciated more than I can say was the special support and critical encouragement of Sarah Davis Smith.

The writing was finished during my Fellowship in October and November of 1976 at the College of Preachers in Washington, D.C. I am most grateful to the Warden of the College, Clement

W. Welsh, and to Earl Brill, Barry Evans, and the entire staff for providing me with a delightful, civilized, beautiful, peaceful, inspiring and scholarly atmosphere in which to bring my project to a close.

Ruth Tiffany Barnhouse
Cambridge, Massachusetts
December 1, 1976

I

SCIENCE AND VALUES

1
The Relation between "What Is" and "What Ought To Be"

*H*uman beings are distinguished from the rest of the animal kingdom by the fact that they experience a disparity between *what is* and *what ought to be*. The whole history of civilization and of what we usually call "progress" depends on that fact. It is related to the faculty of imagination combined with the very protracted time sense which characterizes human consciousness. In even the most "primitive" culture there is at least a rudimentary sense of history: some ritual or legend embodies the beginning of things, there are stories about ancestors, a sense of the "right" way of growth and development, cautionary tales illustrating the cost of mistakes, some attempt to account for things gone wrong and some method of getting them back on course again. In other words, the origin and the goal of human life, the presence of good and evil, and some plan for human adaptation to the conditions of existence are universal issues. Of course they have been perceived and conceptualized in a great variety of ways, and the specific answers evolved by one individual, group or culture often directly contradict the answers evolved by others. But no matter how varied the answers, the underlying questions are the same.

Until very recently in human history it never occurred to anyone to think about these questions in purely secular terms. Philosophers and natural scientists did not pursue their disciplines apart from their religion, nor did theologians confine themselves to speculation about divinity. But these things have taken a radically new turn, which began in the West with the gradual development of the modern, empirical, scientific method. The form this took was that of warfare between science and theology. There were preliminary border incidents, as in all wars, but the eruption to open hostility may fairly be given the date of 1633. In that year Galileo was tried by the Holy Inquisition for publishing and teaching his discoveries, which incontrovertibly established the truth of Copernicus' earlier treatise proposing a heliocentric (as opposed to a geocentric) planetary system. Two hundred ninety-three years later, in 1926, the famous "monkey trial" occurred in Tennessee. William Jennings Bryan prosecuted and Clarence Darrow defended John Scopes, a teacher who had taught Darwin's theory of evolution to his high school class. Darrow made Bryan's defense of the traditional theological interpretation of the creation story in Genesis seem ludicrous in the eyes of most of the world. Many people do not realize that Darrow lost the case. It is only since 1967 that it has been legal to teach evolution in Tennessee, and even now it may not be taught as established fact, but only as a suggested hypothesis, side by side with the theory of special creation.

Around the turn of the century Andrew White, the great scholar who was the first president of Cornell University, published a monumental two-volume work entitled *A History of the Warfare of Science with Theology in Christendom.* Looking at it now, it is almost impossible to realize that such arguments were taking place as recently as a hundred years ago. In England, heresy trials were instituted, not only in ecclesiastical, but in secular courts (since in that country Church and State are not separated) against various scholarly clergy who dared to suggest that the newly developed techniques of historical analysis and criticism of ancient documents should be applied to the Bible. Nowadays, of course, theological debate continues, but it is no longer central to the cultural consciousness even of the general academic community, much less of the people at large. Occasionally some dramatic theological argument tickles the fancy of a reporter for *Time,* and we may read a condescending or sensationalized account, often wildly inaccurate, of something such as the "death of God." But it is extremely rare for anyone outside the theological community to have even the faintest conception of what the contemporary issues in theology are, and the entire religious enterprise is most frequently viewed as a cumbersome and anachronistic system for encouraging people to be "good."

In the 1860s and 1870s things were vastly different. Most British scholars, regardless of their secular field of competence, had taken Holy Orders, and many American scholars were clergymen as well. Theological debate was therefore not insulated, as it is today, from the general concerns of the academic community; all scholarly issues were considered theologically as well as more narrowly and specifically. In a celebrated case of the period (described in detail in White's book), the Anglican Bishop Colenso, a renowned scholar and author in the field of mathematics, wrote a book in 1862 suggesting that the Pentateuch contained numerous historical and scientific inaccuracies. He was excommunicated and Queen Victoria's illustrious, liberal Prime Minister, William Gladstone, prepared the case against him for the courts. But that was not all. The issue agitated the imagination of the entire populace to the point where he was socially ostracized, presented to the public as an "infidel" and a "traitor." His servants left him and people even set their dogs on him! Eventually he was vindicated, and by the 1890s the weight of scholarly evidence had brought about a permanent change in the climate of opinion.

The damage, however, was done. The spectacle of church dignitaries engaging in personal vilification of responsible scholars, with the level of argument often redolent of intellectual hypocrisy, was hardly inspiring or edifying to young and alert minds going through the universities at the time. The case of Bertrand Russell (born in 1872) is poignantly instructive. His book, *Why I Am Not A Christian,* contains fifteen brilliant, bitter essays written over a period of more than half a century. The introduction, which he wrote in 1957, shows clearly that he never recovered from his childhood impressions of religion. He perceived it not only as untrue, but as actively harmful to people's growth and damaging to their social and personal ethics. He never knew that religion might be in any significant way designed to assist humankind in relating to the transcendent areas of Ultimate

Concern, or in holding up a luminous vision of *what ought to be* and helping us along the painful way to that distant goal. Nevertheless, Russell was passionately concerned with such questions, as the following quotation reveals:

> The center of me is always and eternally a terrible pain—a curious wild pain—a searching for something beyond what the world contains, something transfigured and infinite, the beatific vision—God—I do not find it, I do not think it is to be found—but the love of it is my life—it's like passionate love for a ghost. At times it fills me with rage, at times with wild despair, it is the source of gentleness and cruelty and work, it fills every passion that I have—it is the actual spring of life in me.[1]

The alienation of such a mind and heart is a terrible indictment against the Church. And the way in which this came about is, I believe, the most important reason why the Church is considered irrelevant today by much of the secular society.

Theologians overstepped their bounds and encroached on the proper territory of science—to discover as much as possible about *what is.* They forgot that their own mandate is the formation and nourishment of the soul, the training and encouragement of people to be citizens of the City of God whose boundaries are those of the universe and whose time frame is not time at all, but eternity. Their great sacrilege was in reducing the significance and terms of reference of the sacred myths and divine revelations to the narrow dimensions of the human sensory-intellectual apparatus. The motive for this sacrilege is Luciferian pride, which wants to usurp the Center, to dethrone God and put a creature in his place. The substitute creature has not always been Man himself. Often, with less honesty, it has been a mini-God of Man's own devising, a mini-God limited by Man's rational capacity to describe and envision Him. The method of the sacrilege is stupidity—the old story of the Tower of Babel expresses it well.

Even fifty years ago I would not have had to retell that story; no one could have been educated to the point of being able to read this book without already knowing it. But for those of you whose teachers foolishly imagined that the old lore was dispensable superstition, it tells of a time when the people of the world, wishing to "make a name for themselves," decided to build a city with a tower reaching up to heaven. As though they *could!* Before this, they all spoke the same language; perhaps that is why they began to imagine that they understood and knew so much, and developed delusions of grandeur. In any case, God must have thought so because His way of bringing their overly ambitious building project to a halt was to come down and miraculously arrange it so that they no longer spoke in one language but in many, and no one could understand any tongue but their own.

Unfortunately, theologians completely missed the point of this story and supposed that their special training and ecclesiastical status constituted an intellectual tower actually reaching to an understanding of heaven. The sun could not, they said, be the center of the solar system because humankind resides on Earth. God *must* have put people at the real center of things so Galileo was wickedly wrong. The earth must have been created in seven literal days, and the creatures, including man and woman, at one stroke. So the geologists and Darwin must be wickedly wrong. They knew all there was to know about guilt and sin, and especially about sex; they were not prepared to admit that *any* of Man's ways of thinking about God could be based on anthropomorphic projections. So Freud must be wickedly wrong.

The result of this intellectual pride is plain, and precisely the same as that outlined in the original parable of Babel. Christianity is no longer a unified body of believers who understand one another and can communicate freely. It is divided into many groups of people, some of whom do not even acknowledge that others are Christians at all! And it is only within living memory that any Christians have been willing to concede publicly that those who worship God under other names or through other myths are not wickedly deluded and destined for eternal damnation. This unseemly and divisive spectacle, still too often enlivened by ignorant posturing and pretensions or deadened by castrated sentimentality in the face of the vigors and terrors of life and death, continues to widen the gulf of misunderstanding and contempt which separates Christians from "the world."

What is intellectual pride? It is a failure of judgment and of imagination, and is the only possible result for those whose need for control renders them incapable of tolerating either uncertainty or change, let alone mystery. Of course we are reaping the whirlwind of those errors. Our arrogant turn-of-the-century optimism about "progress" has been shattered by wars and wickedness on an unprecedented and terrifying scale. The verdict of irrelevance has been brought against Christianity by those who found its credibility fatally impaired by several centuries of inappropriate meddling with *what is* instead of attending to its proper sphere of concern: *what ought to be.* The human species not only knows, but evaluates. We are not only *homo sapiens,* but *homo judicans.* Both functions are a given, inescapable part of our humanity, and both can be contaminated by ignorance. We have spent so much time focusing on the very real dangers of intellectual ignorance and misinformation that we have all but forgotten the dangers of moral ignorance and misinformation. As I have indicated, this sorry state of affairs has been brought about by the ill-conceived interference of theologians with questions of empirical fact to the detriment of their true functions—cherishing the vision of the ideal, the perception of mystery, and the investigation and cultivation of value systems. But, because of our basic two-fold human constitution, we continue to make judgments all the time, however badly and however limited our ability to do so may be due to poor training, superstition, or mistaken premises. Religious education at the level of most Sunday schools, or even the average sermon, is a joke. Rules of conduct are taught superstitiously, which is to say, in a manner forgetful of the meaning or purpose of the rules. And people will no longer subscribe to a moral code which rests on such premises as avoiding the wrath of God, or securing benefits in a static and boring hereafter —especially not in a time which has seen the wrathful hells of Auschwitz and the siege of Leningrad, Vietnam and the firebombing of Dresden, as well as the culprits of Watergate getting rich on the royalties from their memoirs. If there is any consistent, effective, secular system of moral education in the West, I have not heard of it.

Nevertheless, in spite of this bill of particulars against the theological establishment, capitulation to the scientific enterprise is only getting us out of the frying pan and into the fire. Knowledge, however elaborate and sophisticated, is simply not enough. We are substituting facts for truth, expertise for wisdom. The moral chaos which is rapidly resulting has now reached proportions which are alarming to all but the most cynical. We continue to choose, to value one thing above another, simply because we cannot avoid it; this is our human nature, but we are clearly choosing very badly. People who have decided that the Devil is imaginary and God, if not actually dead, is at least out to lunch, must invent some new system for deciding how to behave. The warfare between science and theology provided some dramatic spectacles, and the common human tendency to back winners has caused most people to turn to science to fill the leadership gap left by the decline of religion. The scientists, however, would do well to study the history of theology's decline if they do not wish to be condemned to suffer the same fate.

Theology got into trouble from which it has not yet recovered by arrogating to itself the right to decide *what is,* and science is now in danger of making the obverse error of believing that it has the necessary competence to decide *what ought to be.* Attempts to infer values from the results of scientific investigations can also be shown to embody a logical fallacy. No discovery has ever contained any clue as to whether or how it should be used. Surely, someone might object, the discovery that penicillin was lethal to certain bacteria clearly implied that it ought to be given to people suffering from diseases caused by those bacteria. No. That implication does not come from anything known about penicillin or bacteria or disease, but from our prior value judgment that disease ought not to be.

The issue is considerably more complex when it comes to attempts on the part of psychology and other behavioral sciences to explain various aspects of what used to be called "moral faculties." But the principle is exactly the same as in the simpler example about penicillin given above. C. S. Lewis, in a reference to Freud's theory of the origin of guilt, explains this very well:

. . . attempts to resolve the moral experience into something else always presuppose the very thing they are trying to explain—as when a famous psychoanalyst deduces it from prehistoric parricide. If the parricide produced a sense of guilt, that was because men felt they ought not to have committed it: if they did not so feel, it could produce no sense of guilt. Morality, like numinous awe, is a jump; in it, man goes beyond anything that can be "given" in the facts of experience.[2]

Physicists in this century have demonstrated that there is no such thing as complete scientific objectivity, since the observer's mere presence, not to mention whatever intervention may be involved in a particular experiment, always changes the conditions and thus affects the results, however slightly. If this is true even in the natural sciences, it becomes immensely more significant in the behavioral sciences, especially in psychology. Here the object of study is the human mind, and the instrument with which we must make the study is another human mind.

In one way, of course, this is an advantage. The common humanity of the observer and the observed makes subtle, empathetic understanding possible. But it also makes the distance required for a thoroughly objective overview impossible. For example, behavioral scientists studying persons from their own culture have the drawbacks of being in some ways too close to the subject. On the other hand, anthropologists studying members of a completely different culture, while able to get a better overview, run the risk of misinterpretation due to inability to "get inside" the experience of their subjects.

These problems in accurate observation are greatly compounded by the difficulties inherent in learning to distinguish one's observations from one's conclusions. Again, this comes back to the fact that it is impossible even to imagine a human being without a value system. People who have no value system beyond that of catering, at whatever cost to others, to their own needs and wishes, are usually unable to function in society—or else society is unable to function around them —and are technically referred to as "psychopaths." But even that primitive psychological organization centers on a value judgment: "I come first, no matter what." Since language is not merely our most powerful tool but also the most powerful and imaginative symbol of experience, knowing and valuing are inextricably mixed in nearly all of our patterns of speech. For instance, the difference between "stubborness" and "persistence" lies not in the behavior itself, but in how that repetitive behavior is valued by the observer. On the other hand, the difference between "investigation" and "meddling" may lie in the way an observer's behavior is valued by the subject.

c.f.

The technical jargon of science has been specifically designed to solve this problem by attempting to find impartial, disinterested, and value-free ways of describing phenomena. The reason this is often hard to understand and sometimes even offensive is because this denial of values goes against our natural grain. When the method is applied to the description of human behavior, as, for example, in the original Kinsey report, one immediately gets the impression that something very important has been left out. Since values are intimately involved in every human activity, particularly in the case of sexuality, it is not possible to describe any behavior in that area except in the shallowest terms if one is deliberately excluding value considerations. This is true not only in terms of the subjects of the investigation, but also in terms of the investigators—their values are almost impossible to exclude entirely from the research process.

One of the subtler ways in which hidden value assumptions creep into scientific reports is the result of transposing the empirical methods of the natural sciences to the study of human behavior. In geology, for instance, if it is found that in a certain part of the world nearly all of the rock formations have a particular composition and character, it is perfectly proper to conclude that this formation is natural or normal for that region. Such conclusions are arrived at mainly on statistical grounds. In general, the methods of science are designed to deal with those phenomena which either recur frequently in nature or which can be reproduced in the laboratory for repeated study. Up to a point, these methods are entirely appropriate in dealing with human beings, especially when the aspect under study is primarily physical. In the medical sphere, health is defined as the absence of disease. But this is emphatically not true in the spheres of psychology and social behavior. Here health is intimately bound up with the questions of meaning and value. Statistics are of no help here. Yet I have read many articles in behavioral science journals which report that, for example, twenty-one percent of the studied population is engaged in some conventionally disapproved behavior such as wife-swapping. The completely illogical conclusion will be that since so many are doing it, it must be "normal," and it is therefore time to revise the moral code.

The investigators believe they have been objective because they have used scientific methods to disclose some new information about *what is*. Up to this point they are right. But suppose instead that public health officials had discovered that in a certain community twenty-one percent of the population had cholera. They would certainly not conclude that because so many had it, cholera must be normal. They would realize they were faced with an epidemic and would immediately take steps to eradicate it. This would be because there would be no doubt in their minds that cholera ought not to be. It is not possible to assign meaning to *what is* except in terms of *what ought to be*, and we do this all the time even when we are not aware of it. In the examples cited—twenty-one percent of a population wife-swapping and twenty-one percent of a population having cholera —it is easy to see that the meaning of these findings and decisions on what, if anything, should be done about them rests on the investigators' prior beliefs about *what ought to be*. Researchers who illogically state that, since wife-swapping is prevalent it is therefore acceptable, are not making a contribution to science, but are only disclosing something about their own personal value system.

For the last several years there has been an increasing number of sessions at the annual meeting of the American Psychiatric Association devoted to various ethical issues. These sessions are extremely well attended, often drawing over a thousand listeners. In 1976 there was a three-hour panel about the growing problem of sexual interaction between therapists and their patients. In spite of some claims from the fringes of the profession that this sort of thing may be not only harmless, but actually therapeutic, the panelists were unanimously opposed to such behavior. Yet during the discussion period, when a questioner tried to elicit the basis for the disapproval of one of the panelists (a prestigious professor of psychiatry at a great medical school) the professor was unable to go beyond the evidence that it either impedes therapy or aggravates the patient's condition or both. When asked whether he would change his mind if some comprehensive research project demonstrated that there were no harmful psychological effects, he (with visible reluctance) said that, yes, under those circumstances he might have to alter his opinion. Apparently his value system is not sufficiently articulated to enable him to distinguish the growing edge from the lunatic fringe.

Unfortunately, this kind of error is being made with increasing frequency, and, in the name of science, we are being pushed into the dangerous and unworkable position of making statistics the basis of morality. This error is compounded by a misinterpretation of the principle of tolerance whereby we are rapidly drifting to a climate in which no opinion or course of action is intrinsically valued above any other.* It is with pain and difficulty that humanity has gradually evolved to a point where individual conscience and responsibility are valued. These are the indispensable prerequisites of freedom, and it is at our great peril that we allow the emergence of any system which attacks or erodes them. The result, inevitably, is mass-mindedness and collective regression. Far from the destructive circularity inherent in the notion that *what is* probably is *what ought to be,* mature humanity requires not only objective knowledge, but also the ability to imagine consequences and alternatives to *what is.* These consequences and alternatives must be seriously evaluated before decisions are made if we are to have any hope of exercising control over our lives or influencing our future in a constructive direction. But, evaluated against what standard? Clearly, to take any merely statistical view as the ultimate standard is very dangerous and leads straight to that mass-

*Tolerance, properly understood, does not entail abandonment of standards; it does entail great clarity about the difference between *exposing to* and *imposing on* others one's own view of truth.

mindedness which we want to avoid. It is not safe to do this even in a community of people whom we intuitively and unconsciously perceive to be decent, right-thinking citizens. If we have formed the habit, even in such favorable circumstances, of measuring *our* conduct exclusively against the standard of *others'* conduct, we are asking for trouble. We are then easy prey to those demagogues or propaganda merchants who have mastered the evil art of subtly manipulating public opinion for their own ends, who know how to tempt us to evaluate the new, not in terms of *what ought to be,* but in terms of *what is "in."*

That scientists, who fought so valiantly for so long to rescue us from the superstitions and oppressions resulting from the abuses of theology, should now be endangering humanity in so similar a way is truly ironic. If it was a bad thing to pursue the study of how to make judgments in a manner which ignored the empirical facts, it may be even worse to idolize facts to the exclusion of the process of conscience-based decision-making. An old proverb says that God looks after fools and little children (the ignorant); but I doubt if God's approach to the irresponsible learned would be so gentle. If we are to avoid the punishment of eradicating our species with our sophisticated know-how, we have no time to lose in facing the fact that know-how without know-what is ultimately perilous. Scientists, no less than theologians, need to understand the parable of the Tower of Babel.

In a wonderful little book called *The Undiscovered Self,* the great Swiss psychiatrist Carl Jung persuasively argues that religion is the only ultimate protection against mass-mindedness.[3] It is imperative that each person have a reference point outside the self, beyond the limitations of human consciousness. Traditionally this reference point has been given the name of God. But those who do not find the established institutions of religion or the mysterious and paradoxical symbolism of theologies helpful need not be excluded; the essence of religion does not depend on these things, even though they are of inestimable value to those fortunate enough to be able to believe in them. Nevertheless, it seems to me that those who choose to ignore the wisdom painstakingly accumulated over thousands of years may find that their undertaking is lonely and inordinately difficult, and in the end they may only have re-invented the wheel. I am sure this is an important reason why many people return to some practice of religion in their mature years. The persuasive, pragmatic world of popularized twentieth-century science which lured them away from church or temple in their youth proves eventually inadequate, and they find that they cannot satisfactorily relate to the unseen alone. But, with or without the community support of formal religion, it is imperative that spirit and conscience be trained in the religious art of imaginative discourse with that larger principle of reality which includes truth and wisdom as well as facts. This practice alone can bring true independence and freedom, which is far more than just doing what you feel like doing from moment to moment. Those who are truly free have the courage not only to be in the minority, but to stand alone. They also have the humility to remember that being part of a statistically significant group, or even in the majority, does not make them right.

How do these reflections contribute to an understanding of the proper relationship between science and religion? How can these essential disciplines become fruitful partners? Is either of them primary in any sense?

I believe it is not possible to implement religious principles effectively—sometimes not even possible to ask the right questions—without knowing the state of the scientific art. If theology ignores the findings of the human sciences, it runs the risk of setting irrelevant or impossible standards of conduct, and therefore deteriorates into a system for stimulating neurotic guilt in its adherents. The other risk, even if the first is avoided, is that it may give foolish or unworkable directions about how to get to "ought" because it is ignorant of the true starting point, the "is." Science is indeed primary, but only in the technical sense that it should come first, not, as has been assumed recently, in the sense of being most important. In that sense—importance—religion is primary since, as we have seen, it is not possible to assign meaning to the data of experience without a future-oriented value system. There will always be tension between these two ways of dealing with the human condition, if only because of inertia. It is easier to settle for the familiar and to believe in the reality and importance of the visible than it is to work for change toward an uncertainly envisaged future goal.

Nevertheless, it is clear that in the long run we must learn to use both scientific and religious categories in thinking about every issue. What are the facts? What is right? Neither question is as easy to answer as some vocal adherents of each discipline would have us believe, especially when it is asked apart from the other. Rosemary Haughton has said that "theology cannot be conducted in an intellectual laboratory."[4] I believe it is equally true that science cannot be done in a spiritual vacuum. Fruitful cooperation between the two disciplines is possible and, fortunately, is now under way in some quarters. But more, much more, needs to be done.

II

"WHAT IS"

2
History and Anthropology

The word *homosexuality* has been used in so many ways that, unless one realizes that different authors use it to refer to different ideas and behavior patterns, the extensive literature on the subject can seem confusing and contradictory. I shall begin, therefore, by explaining as clearly as possible how I propose to use it in this book.

First of all, homosexuality is not an abstraction that has independent existence, although many write and talk as though it could somehow be detached from people. What is at issue here is the distinction between a *concept* and a *behavior pattern*. This distinction is important because conceptual generalizations about behavior always falsify particular experiences to some extent.

Let me offer an illustration. In the last fifty years or so a great deal of valuable research has been done on child development. A number of experts have believed that knowing something about this work might be helpful to parents, and a series of popular books such as those by Drs. Spock and Ginnott have resulted. However, there is a right way and a wrong way for parents to use this material. The right way is for them to read the book and store the new information in the back of their minds, mostly in the form of improved insight into the general nature of childhood. Then, from this better vantage point, the parents proceed to deal with their children naturally and spontaneously. Their attention is focused on the child, not on the book. But with the wrong way, their attention is focused on the book, not the child. The book becomes in their minds some immutable standard which their children must live up to, or perhaps surpass. This can lead to some very silly parenting. For instance, if it is said that boys begin to display aggressive behavior at around eighteen months, parents may greet their little son's attack on his baby sister only as a reassuring sign that he is normal, and so fail to deal with this behavior appropriately. While it can be helpful to know something about childhood aggressiveness, one must not lose sight of the specific context in which a particular aggressive act takes place or the larger set of circumstances, including the child's personality and energy level. Without this focus on the unique shape of the individual instance, misinterpretations and bad decisions are likely.

Much that is written about homosexuality loses sight of this kind of distinction. As a concept, homosexuality has very limited usefulness, if only because so many different behavior patterns have, at one time or another, been called by that name. In addition, it often gets used to convey not only a description of behavior, but also the way in which that behavior is valued. This becomes even clearer if one considers some of the alternate terms now in common use.

Activist organizations do not use the word *homosexual,* preferring the term *gay,* which is applied to both men and women. Instead of speaking about homosexuality, they have invented the term *gayness.* These ways of referring to their condition are seen as less clinical, more pleasant, not having the negative connotations associated with the standard terminology. Is this true?

Where does the word *gay* come from? *The Oxford English Dictionary* tell us that in the twelfth century it meant mirthful or merry; by the fourteenth century it was also used to mean bright-colored or showy. In the sixteenth century its meaning—brilliant or attractive— was sometimes extended to refer to specious reasoning—that which sounds good but does not stand up to closer scrutiny. By the seventeenth century it began to mean "addicted to social pleasures and dissipations" and was also used as a euphemism for "of immoral life." In the nineteenth century it meant airy, offhand, or light-hearted and was a complimentary adjective if used about women, but not about men. When I was living in New York City during the 1940s the word *gay,* in theater and nightclub circles, was used to designate effeminate male homosexuals. Homosexual men who were not effeminate often felt insulted if they were called gay. It was definitely not a compliment. Apparently the word has undergone further changes in the past thirty years. Nevertheless, I find it puzzling that official homosexual organizations attempting to present a positive public image should choose a word with this history.

There are several words in common usage which employ the prefix *homo.* This comes from the Greek word meaning same and occurs in other English words such as *homogeneous.* This prefix carries no implication of gender. It is a common error to suppose that it is derived from the Latin word *homo.* That word does not mean male, the Latin term for man in that sense being *vir,* but refers to the whole human species. Those who invent and use new words in the service not only of the homosexual movement but also the women's liberation movement, seem to be largely unaware of these distinctions.

Homosexual, therefore, literally means sexual proclivities toward those the same as oneself. *Homophile,* used as a synonym, is puzzling since there are no sexual implications. The Greek word *philea* means affectionate regard, friendship, amiability, or the natural force which unites discordant elements or movements. Of the several Greek words describing relations of attraction between people, this is the least intimate and has no sexual overtones. *Homophilia,* then, means friendship or amiability toward persons the same as oneself—not, I should have thought, anything to make a special point of. *Homophobia* is another recently coined word which is intended to designate, but in fact does not, the attitude of being against homosexuality. The Greek root is *phobos,* which means fear, dread, or terror. The new word, then, really means irrational fear of those who are the same as oneself!

Leaving aside the factor of inaccuracy verging on the illiterate, one sees that all of these alternate terms are intended to convey a different value judgment of the behavior in question than that which has been current in society up to now. Out of respect not only for the English language but also, as is plain from the foregoing discussion of etymology, for homosexuals themselves, I confine myself to the standard terminology.

I use the word *homosexuality* to refer to an *adult* adaptation characterized by *preferential* sexual behavior between members of the same sex. The emphasis on *adult* is extremely important. Much of today's rhetoric does not allow for the fact that adolescence is often accompanied by a period of transitional anxiety or confusion about sexual identity. That observation long antedates any discoveries by modern depth psychologies. To lump discussion of homosexual phenomena in teen-agers together with those occurring in adults is such an inappropriate confusion of disparate categories as to render meaningful discourse virtually impossible.

The definition's emphasis on *preferential* is also important. This is because of those sexually segregated situations where lack of an opposite-sex partner rather than preference for a same-sex partner is the principal factor contributing to the behavior. These include prisons, the military, some kinds of expeditions or frontier situations where there are few if any women, and the like. Depending on what provisions are made for relaxed, natural contact with young people of the opposite sex, non-coeducational boarding schools and colleges may also fall into this category.

It is also important to distinguish the *homosexual act* from *homosexual identification*. In the United States as well as much of the rest of Western culture, any voluntary homosexual act is assumed to reflect a disturbance in sexual identity. As we shall see, this is not the case everywhere. The homosexual act is obvious; people are either having physical sexual relations or they are not. Homosexual identification, on the other hand, signifies a self-concept and a subsequent pattern of relationships which fails to match the individual's (or the culture's) idea of appropriate gender behavior. That the act and the identification are distinct can be seen by the fact that they may occur independently of one another. There are many people whose subjective experience of themselves is homosexual, with conscious sexual attraction to members of their own sex, who nevertheless have, for religious or social reasons, committed no homosexual acts. Less common in this culture are those situations in which certain homosexual acts may be performed without homosexual identification.

These definitions and distinctions must be borne in mind when considering historical and anthropological evidence about the prevalence or incidence of homosexuality, as well as cultural attitudes toward it in other times and places. An excellent starting place for readers wishing to examine the evidence for themselves is Arno Karlen's *Sexuality and Homosexuality.* This book is the result of five years of detailed study of every conceivable aspect of the topic. It does not sacrifice scholarly standards, and yet is written to be fully available to the general reader. The excellent critical bibliography includes both general and technical references. In addition, there are many transcripts of taped interviews, both with various research workers and with homosexuals themselves. The book is an indispensable basic text and reference work for anyone who wants or needs to know more about homosexuality than can be learned either from activists or specialists in one facet or another of this condition. No other source contains a thorough survey of all that is known from the standpoint of every discipline which could possibly contribute to an understanding of homosexuality. Not only that, but, as the title suggests, the author knows that attitudes and facts about homosexuality are inseparable from attitudes and facts about sexuality in general. This is an extremely important point, one frequently overlooked by those proposing that homosexuality be accepted as a normal alternate lifestyle as well as by many who oppose that view. Karlen says:

Those with the scholarly ability to study sexual history effectively have usually shunned it leaving it to the irresponsible, inept, or partisan. . . . If we apply the same rigorous historical tests to documents on the history of sex as we do in other areas of history, our body of knowledge is much smaller than most people think. . . . Every scientist, journalist and common citizen knew all about American sex behavior—until the Kinsey reports left no one unsurprised in some way. If we know so little about our own society, we know a thousand times less about the past. We can only make cautious inferences from snatches of literature and chronicle, as one would from the scattered patches of an almost obliterated fresco. While doing so, it is good to bear in mind the picture of our society that would emerge if posterity dug up from the ruins of a bombed city only *The Scarlet Letter* or *Sanctuary* or the poems of Emily Dickinson and Genet's *The Balcony*.[1]

After issuing this warning, he devotes 170 pages to a meticulous review of the available literary and historical evidence. Some of his conclusions are surprising, running contrary to much of the contemporary rhetoric.

Most people believe that homosexuality was the ideal in ancient Greece, widely accepted and practiced. This view is a great oversimplification. There was no mention of it in Homer: in the *Iliad* and the *Odyssey*, Achilles and Patroclus were comrades, nothing more, and Ganymede was really only Zeus' cupbearer, not his *catamite* (young, male prostitute). It was not until the homosexual apologists of the Classical period began to rewrite the old lore in an attempt to justify their own behavior that such practices were ever attributed to the ancient gods and heroes. By that time, the position of women in upper class Greece had deteriorated badly. The deep, enduring relationships characterized both by eroticism and friendship between husband and wife, which Homer described so movingly, were no longer believed to be either ideal or possible. Women of good family were not educated, nor were they encouraged to cultivate their spirit in any way. Not surprisingly, they were also sexually uninteresting. The *hetaira*, or female prostitutes, were an exception, being not only erotically but also intellectually competent. It was in this kind of social atmosphere that the notorious Greek homosexuality flourished.

Even at its peak, it was considered deviant by most, and was officially illegal everywhere except in the city of Elis. Those who praised it were in the minority, a leisured literary, or sometimes military, elite. The plays of Aristophanes treat it with withering contempt, and this attitude reflected the opinion of the majority of citizens. In his later years, Plato himself condemned it as unnatural and degrading.

In the much publicized circles in which homosexuality flourished, it was limited to that form known as pederasty, which means love of boys. Grown men were ridiculed if they played the receptive sexual role, which was always assigned to the younger partner whose age was between puberty and twenty years at most. After that age, men were expected to marry, this being required by law in many places. In addition to their procreative duties at home, adult males had sexual relations with hetaira or catamites, or had a particular affair with a young male protégé from a good family. Grown men did not ordinarily have sexual relations with other adult males; when this happened it was considered ludicrous and perverse. This overall pattern of sexual behavior did not conflict with masculine gender role expectations. "To the bisexual Greek, women and boys were both 'the ones who are fucked,' submissive nonmales."[2]

In the same way that the homosexual apologists of Classical Greece revised the original legends of Homer, those of today have made it increasingly fashionable to assert that most of the great Renaissance artists and writers were homosexual. There is no real evidence to document these claims, even for Michelangelo and Leonardo da Vinci, much less for Shakespeare. In keeping with the conventional flowery style of neo-Classical poetry which glorified and romanticized male friendships, Michelangelo in his old age wrote some poems to young men (but also to a woman, Vittoria Colonna); this is the *only* evidence for his alleged homosexuality. There is no record that he ever had a sexual affair with anyone, male or female. Speculation that an artist was homosexual based on such indirect literary "evidence" not biographically substantiated in any way, was first used by Oscar Wilde (hardly a disinterested observer) to impugn Shakespeare. This method overlooks the fact that there is a strong body of evidence suggesting that the WH of the sonnets was an imaginary person, invented for rhetorical purposes. It also overlooks the fact that the attitude toward homosexuality expressed in the plays is strongly negative. Interested readers are referred to recent books by the great Elizabethan scholar, Alfred Leslie Rowse, which, drawing on newly discovered material, definitively refute the homosexual claims about Shakespeare.[3]

On the other hand, there are reliable historical records showing that Francis Bacon was homosexual, yet no trace of this appears in his writings. Still, the idea that the sexual habits of artists can be deduced through their work has persisted, encouraged recently by psychoanalysts using this method in support of the questionable idea of "latent homosexuality." Such work by Freud over a half-century ago, and since repudiated both as to method and content by all but a few die-hard orthodox Freudians, is the *only* evidence to support the notion of Leonardo da Vinci's homosexual tendencies.

More recently, homosexual apologists, while repudiating most of classical psychoanalysis, have continued the practice of drawing personal biographical inferences from works of art in an apparent attempt to arrogate to themselves a substantial portion, if not the lion's share, of the world's creativity. There is no evidence whatsoever to support such claims. In fact, contemporary psychological research shows that on tests designed to measure creativity and divergent thinking, heterosexuals tend to perform better than homosexuals.[4] And yet, to give only one example, a recent issue of *The Art Bulletin* contained an article which purported to demonstrate Donatello's homosexuality from his beautiful bronze statue of the young David. The same article attempted to add to the growing number of inuendoes suggesting that various biblical personages were homosexual.[5] David and Jonathan, Jesus and John the beloved disciple, are the best known instances. But this merely continues, in modern dress, the Classical Greek habit of eroticizing friendship. This attitude does both true eroticism and true friendship a considerable disservice.

Professor John Dixon has brilliantly refuted not only this particular attempt but also has exposed the slipshod pseudo-scholarship behind which this variety of polemic masquerades. The first questionable premise is that it is possible to recognize homosexuals by posture and body type. Not only is this rarely true, but it is an assertion which homosexuals themselves usually deny. Secondly, Donatello produced statues and paintings of hundreds of different subjects. One would hardly attempt to infer, for instance, that a statue of a woman was evidence that he was female! There are also more technical artistic grounds for rejecting such arguments, involving the nature of symbolism and similar considerations.[6]

After reviewing all the evidence, Karlen concludes that the incidence of homosexuality among the artists and writers of the Renaissance was lower than the incidence in the rest of the educated classes. However, the notion that creativity and male homosexuality are linked remains in the public imagination, and in some instances may even have the force of a self-fulfilling prophecy. A boy with artistic talent who is told often enough that this is a sign of homosexual tendencies may believe it and eventually act on it, especially if the rest of his upbringing is equally benighted.

In the United States today there are some artistic professions which do seem to attract a higher percentage of homosexuals than do other professions. The reasons for this are complex, but by no means limited to the question of talent. Artists have always been relatively less conventional in every way and more tolerant of the foibles of others. In a society which persecutes homosexuals, the artistic world offers a haven of sorts. Furthermore, once positions of influence have been achieved, there is a clear tendency to prefer hiring other homosexuals. This is not only because of the understandable and humane wish to assist fellow outcasts, but also because of the preference of many to band together in what has been called the "homosexual collective."

The current wave of books, magazines, movies, and other public entertainment which would have been banned as obscene only a few years ago is not without precedent. In the eighteenth century a similar situation existed in England, as it had in Rome fifteen centuries earlier. During both periods the apparent increase in homosexuality was part of a more general outbreak of unconventional sexual behavior. In England these deviations, largely occurring in the upper classes so far as can be ascertained, inspired amusement, anger or disgust in most people, and the legal penalties remained severe, especially for homosexuality.

The history of sexuality, insofar as we can infer anything remotely accurate from the uneven, sparse and partisan nature of the available records, seems to be characterized by alternating eras of strictness and licentiousness. But it would be misleading to stop there, since these fluctuations have been more at the level of expressed cultural standards than at the level of behavior. In short, they tell us more about what some people were willing, not to say eager, to admit than about what they actually did. The reasons for these variations in standards are complex, but strict eras tend to account for themselves in the rhetoric of reform. Open eras, on the other hand, tend to perceive themselves as light-bearing liberators. Often the social history of the preceding age is highly oversimplified and mythologized in order to provide some rational support for the new ways. The present tendency to use the term "Victorian" as a synonym for extremes of sexual repression is an example. All we really know is that during that era people came to value the appearance of "respectability" very highly; this meant that sexual impulses and behavior were not considered proper for public discussion or display. There is no evidence that this attitude is an accurate reflection of what went on in Victorian bedrooms. The aphorism of the period—"You can do anything you like so long as you don't do it in the street and frighten the horses"—is probably much closer to the truth. In addition, until very recently we have had no record of the behavior patterns of the large mass of society, but only of a small portion of the professional and upper classes. To engage in the more picturesque realms of licentiousness, after all, takes both leisure and money.

There is another curious phenomenon which makes it difficult to know what is actually going on, especially with respect to such strongly taboo behavior as homosexuality. Both those who are against it and those who are for it tend to exaggerate its incidence and to claim that it is on the rise. Conservatives do so in order to sound the alarm and rouse public opinion in favor of stricter sanctions, both social and legal. Apologists do so in order to give the impression of an unstemmable tide of change. There is no hard evidence to support such claims. The actual incidence of homosexuality as defined earlier in this chapter has probably been constant at somewhere between three and five percent of the male population for centuries in Western culture. Current claims by some homosexual organizations of an incidence of ten to fifteen percent are wildly exaggerated, and impossible to substantiate. Not even by including men who have had serious and repeated childhood or adolescent experiences could such figures be approached for the population as a whole.

While female homosexuality has been recorded as far back as Sappho, the famous seventh-century B.C. poet, much less has been written about it, and much of what we have is in the form of pornography written by and for men and is therefore useless in discovering what actually happened between women. Accurate estimates of the incidence are therefore impossible. Whether the paucity of information reflects the fact that most writers have been male, cannot be known for sure. Certainly homosexuality has never been taken as seriously in women as it has in men by society. In most places there have not even been laws enacted against it.

One reason for this has to do with the ancient and medieval ideas of the nature of sexual energy, ideas which persist in many quarters to this day and which are part of the beliefs of many occult systems now enjoying popular revival. The active or positive sexual energy was believed to be male. The female sexual role was seen as the grounding or receiving of this active male principle. This notion has nothing to do with the kind or amount of enjoyment or participation in the actual sexual encounter, but only with the metaphysical concept of the nature of the energies involved. Now it is also part of such beliefs that, if the right techniques are employed, energy can be transmuted from one plane to another. All ceremonial magic depends on this premise, whether "white" or "black." Practitioners of black magic have no scruples about exploiting victims or diverting available energy to the selfish ends of the magician. In the worst forms, sacrifice—usually of chickens or other small animals, less often human infants or children —was employed, because fresh blood was considered a powerful energy source. But much more common was the use of sexual energy. It was secured either by sadistic and "unnatural" heterosexual acts, or, more frequently, by ritual male homosexual acts. The presiding magician made use of the positive sexual energy thus liberated to perform whatever magical operation he had underway. The suppression of the Knights Templar in the fourteenth century was accomplished partly by accusing them of such practices. While male homosexuals have been disapproved of for a wide variety of reasons, it seems likely that the belief in the magical potential of their acts contributed substantially to the centuries-old pattern of virulent persecution which has persisted to the present. People were not only contemptuous of what was perceived as homosexual effeminacy, but were actually afraid of the homosexual's power to do harm. Women, not being thought to possess the kind of energy usable in such magic, were spared the worst excesses of harsh laws and social ostracism. Such laws as there were seem mainly to have been directed against those forms of lesbian practice which employ an artificial phallus. Furthermore, in a strong patriarchy nothing women did merely between themselves was thought particularly significant. Of course, if their sexual behavior interfered with the rights and privileges of men, that was an entirely different story, and here the penalties were harsh indeed.[7]

So far we have considered a few highlights in the history of homosexuality in the West. What about its place in other cultures? According to Karlen, astonishingly little is known about this, and until very recently the only information available was casual and anecdotal. The available information can support conclusions no more extensive than that travelers saw some evidence of homosexual practice in nearly all parts of the world which they visited, but that this was always officially disapproved of, even where there seemed to be flagrant homosexual subcultures.

It is only in this century that the methods of scientific anthropology have been developed; fully reliable methods of sex research are still in the process of elaboration. Anthropologists did not even begin to study homosexuality in other cultures until the 1930s. Karlen reviews all of the available material in his book and emphasizes the inadequacy of the research techniques in all but a few studies. (For example, many do not differentiate homosexual acts from homosexual identification.)

Even worse than this trouble with sources of information is the outright misunderstanding when it comes to the books and articles written for the general public which purport to draw on these sources, especially in the material produced by homosexual apologists. Part of the difficulty comes from the fact that Westerners, be they scientists or not, have been thoroughly imbued with very negative and primitive

attitudes toward homosexuality. Beyond that, Americans in particular have a very strong tendency to see things in black and white. One
is either for or against something; the middle-of-the-road view or the
view that perceives shades of gray is frequently dismissed as "wishy-
washy." The more emotionally laden an issue becomes, the more
likely we Americans are to want to take a simplistic view of it, much
to the amusement (or contempt) of our more sophisticated and experienced European cousins. The result of this tendency in the present
instance is that, unless a culture or tribe imposes severe penalties for
homosexuality, an American observer is likely to assume that the
behavior is accepted. We simply overlook forms of disapproval other
than punishment.

I offer this somewhat elaborate explanation to account for the
oft-heard reports that homosexuality is fully tolerated and even ad-
mired in this or that culture. Without my explanation, I would have
to assume that the authors of such reports are deliberately misrepre-
senting the facts, since no such observation has ever been made by an
anthropologist. It is true, however, that many societies have managed
to find ways of dealing with homosexuality which are far more tolerant and humane, far less cruel and oppressive than ours. From the
available evidence Karlen confidently draws the following conclusion:

> But we do know that predominant or exclusive homosexuality is seen
> negatively everywhere, _and that when a society alleged to approve homosex-_
> _uality is carefully studied, it turns out that homosexual acts are accepted_
> _only in special situations or times of life,_ and to the extent that they do not
> impair heterosexual functioning or loss of sexual identity. Rejection of
> one's sex role can be provided with an institutionalized role, as among the
> Mohave, but that does not imply approval or a happy way of life. Whenever
> the final limits of heterosexuality and biologically appropriate role are
> infringed, the result is sanctions that range from death through persecution
> to harassment and mild contempt.[8]

Much more research needs to be done before many fascinating
questions can be answered about why and how different sexual customs evolve. However, several very important facts have emerged.

Nowhere is there a society without some serious limitation on sex. This always includes a prohibition against incest, at least with the immediate members of the nuclear family if not for more distant relatives as well. Nowhere is indiscriminate promiscuity acceptable, though what pattern of partner selection is considered promiscuous may be defined differently from one society to another. Nowhere is adult reversed gender identity accepted, either for men or for women, but the pattern of technically homosexual acts which must be violated before the pejorative judgment of homosexual identification is made varies widely. As previously stated, societies also differ greatly in the cultural patterns evolved for dealing with such homosexuality as may occur. Finally, there is no relation between the incidence of homosexuality in any of its forms and the more general sexual permissiveness or repressiveness of the culture. It has been observed to occur, but also to be virtually absent, in societies of both kinds.

In the light of these disclosures, it does not seem that an appeal either to history or to culture is likely to be decisive in settling the issue for our own time and place. But we do learn that if the current attempt to declare homosexuality a normal alternate life style succeeds, it will be a first in human civilization.

3
Biology

There is a recurring tendency to equate what is natural with what is good and to suspect that which is artificial of being bad. In our own time this seems to be a reaction against the dehumanizing excesses of technology. It is also the result of the somewhat oversimplified and distorted versions of Freudian theory which have captured the public imagination; these are erroneously understood to teach that repression of instinctive behavior or of emotions is harmful, and to avoid complexes and neurosis it is better to "let it all hang out." Nevertheless, our age is not the first to idealize "nature," Rousseau's romantic notions about the "noble savage" being a case in point.

In practice, even the most ardent proponents of the "natural" make concessions to civilization. At the technological level, most are willing to use automobiles, or at least bicycles, and are happy to drink pasteurized milk, to have their appendix removed by modern surgical techniques or to take penicillin for their pneumonia. At the behavioral level, some limits are always set to untrammeled expression, particularly if violence to person or property is in question.

There is such a wide variety of human temperament and behavior, there are so many different forms of social organization, and the acculturation process begins so young and lasts so long that it is truly impossible to accurately distinguish what is really natural. Beyond those simple acts such as eating and sleeping which are necessary for survival, there are only a few things one can with any certainty point to as unequivocally natural, in the sense of being uninfluenced by the cultural process. People live in community and some form of family is the basic unit of social organization, supported by a prohibition of incest. They also elaborate mythologies as a way of giving meaning to their experience and of justifying or explaining their lifestyle. Beyond this, the diversity is amazing. For instance, some primitive tribes can be found in which interpersonal violence is unknown. In others, the life style seems to be one of constant, angry paranoia, with attack and defense the chief means of communication. Which, if either, can be called natural? Or are both to be thought of as natural?

Perhaps the most important thing to realize about the human species is its almost incredible adaptability to different circumstances and the profligacy of its imagination in devising new ones. Still, it is important to try to discover what the limits of this adaptability may be so that people or cultures are not forced into patterns which would take too great a toll in energy or lead to symptoms of excessive stress.

With animals, things are a little easier. No species of animal shows the wide variability and adaptability which is characteristic of humans. Probably the single most significant reason for this is that they are almost entirely dependent on their biological constitution for survival. This means that the natural environment is more limiting for them than it is for us. They are not able, as we are, to modify their surroundings easily in response either to necessity or imagination. Not only that, but for humans these effects can be cumulative, due to the transmission of culture made possible by language and the prolonged helplessness of the young.

Before the development of modern science, both biological and behavioral, people were confident that they knew what was natural. This confidence, we can now see, was unjustified. The old attitudes are clearly revealed in the wording of some of the laws still on the books in most states which refer to various disapproved sex practices as "unnatural acts." Even the relatively small and inadequate amount of cultural and scientific research into human sexuality upon which any reliance can be placed is sufficient to let us know that almost none of these acts is truly unnatural.

On the other hand, the words *natural* and *unnatural* have undergone a subtle but important change of meaning since the time of their original use. We now understand the words to be saying something about whether or not such acts are performed with any regularity by people who are not noticeably deranged. This is a modern idea derived from the methods of empirical science, including the study of statistics. In former times, the words were used quite differently; they referred to the *nature* of Man as a being endowed with reason and free will and therefore equipped to make moral choices. Acts which were the result of wrong choice, either through ignorance or sin, were considered unnatural in that they were not intended to occur. Such uses of the words *natural* and *unnatural* do not accord with modern consciousness and are, in fact, both misleading and subject to abuse. But the ghost of these meanings lingers on in the tendency to equate the natural with the good mentioned at the beginning of this chapter. What we have done, however, is to reverse the order in which these terms are considered. Formerly one began with a concept of good and deduced the natural from that. Now the natural is first, arrived at by observation of what actually occurs, and the conclusion drawn is: what exists—provided that it involves no physical harm to anyone— defines what is good.

Most people writing about homosexuality seem to rely heavily on the concept that homosexual behavior is natural. They base this not only on historical and cultural material, but also on the idea that homosexual behavior is widespread among animals. The logic of using this kind of information as evidence to support any conclusions about what may be appropriate or desirable in humans has always escaped me. It is natural for many animals, to give but one possible example, to kill and eat their prey in a manner which by human standards is extremely cruel; but nobody uses those facts about natural animal behavior to justify human cruelty. On the contrary, to call someone an animal is a common, idiomatic way of describing a person who is cruel or insensitive to others.

But there is a reason why it may be enlightening to know something about animal behavior, and this has to do with the theory of evolution. Human anatomy and physiology have been found to be continuous with that of our earlier, simpler ancestors. In general, more primitive structures and processes form the nucleus of our more complex organization; rather than being altogether discarded, they are added to or built upon in the course of becoming more elaborate. Because of our different needs and capacities, some things which are functional in the lower mammals are minimally so in humans and exist in forms which are apparently vestigial. A good example of this is body hair, which in animals is an essential protection but in humans is mainly a remnant. The sciences of embryology and comparative anatomy, which rely on an appreciation of these principles, have contributed enormously to the progress of modern medicine. There are good reasons to assume that careful and detailed study of animal behavior may be similarly fruitful in illuminating some of the problematic areas of human behavior.

Let me offer an illustration. There have been systems of child-rearing which view all evidence of aggressiveness, at however young an age, as moral perversity to be rooted out at all costs. But once it is realized that all young male mammals (including the primates, our closest relatives) begin to display aggressiveness at an early age and that this behavior is essential to their survival, the human problem can be seen in a new light. It will be realized that to try to eradicate the aggressiveness is impossible in most instances without doing damage in other ways—the old expression "to break a child's spirit" says it well. Instead, efforts should be directed to training children to use their biologically given aggressive energies in ways which are not destructive to individuals or to society, but rather in ways which could be helpful both to themselves and to the total human enterprise.

Since there is such a scarcity of scientific information about sexuality compared to what is known about other kinds of behavior, we may hope that the study of animals might contribute something to our understanding of ourselves. But this should not be used at the simplistic level of assuming that, because animals do or don't do particular sexual things, humans are therefore justified in doing or not doing likewise. What, then, are the facts as presently known?

The reports about the occurrence of homosexual behavior in animals are conflicting. In part, this is a problem of definition centering around the fact that in animals—as well as in humans, as we shall see —there is a great deal of overlap between sexual signals and behavior and aggressive signals and behavior. Before the last thirty years of ethological research—led by Konrad Lorenz and Nikolaas Tinbergen and, more recently, by Frank Beach and Clellan Ford—this fact was not known, much less understood.

Popular opinion and homosexual apologists to the contrary, in the animal kingdom there is no such thing as homosexual behavior which includes climax or even, between males, intromission. The rare exceptions occur under the extreme circumstances of artificial stress, such as overcrowding of rats in laboratories. The few poorly authenticated reports about animals born and raised in captivity under artificial zoo conditions are worthless, since we now know that these conditions interfere with neo-natal imprinting, programming, and the other natural learning processes by which animals in their normal habitat come to sexual maturity. What observers of animals frequently mistake for homosexuality is actually part of a very elaborate dominant/submissive ritual behavior. When any animal attacks another of the same species, the animal who is losing the fight turns some weaker part of his anatomy toward the aggressor. Wolves, for instance, turn their heads to expose the jugular vein, at which point the fight is over as the loser has conceded the victory. In primates it is common to expose the usually highly-colored buttocks or the genitals as a signal of defeat. These gestures are not sexual; they have no connection with sexual arousal, orgasm, or reproduction.

In addition, animals are often seen to engage in same sex-mounting behavior. This is particularly common in house pets. In an interview with Karlen in the late 1960s, Frank Beach stated that the precise meaning of this behavior is not understood but that "it's questionable that mounting in itself can properly be called sexual."[1] The persistent tendency on the part of observers to interpret such behavior as sexual is an anthropomorphic projection based on two things: the anatomical parts involved in the behavior have sexual significance for humans doing anything similar; and, there is a reductionistic and distorted twentieth-century Western view, at its worst in the United States, which assumes that all physical contact is at least potentially sexual.

On the basis of initial observations, Beach published an article in 1949 which said that homosexual behavior was seen in animals. This article is frequently cited by apologists seeking support for their claim that homosexuality is natural. Typical of these is a recent book, *The Homosexual Matrix,* by C. A. Tripp.[2] This author, himself an avowed homosexual, is a practicing psychologist in New York. His book has been extensively reviewed and widely hailed as a modern sympathetic presentation which avoids the anti-homosexual bias attributed to previous writers on the subject. The unwary reader may not take the trouble to check Tripp's facts and references because this is generally thought to be unnecessary with someone of his apparent professional standing. But there are misrepresentations on nearly every page. For example, on page twenty-six Tripp insists that homosexuality is rampant throughout the animal kingdom. His source is the 1949 article by Beach. Yet his own bibliography includes all of Beach's subsequent work, including that published in 1965 which specifically denies his earlier statement on the basis of further research. Karlen's book is also listed in the bibliography, and that includes the even later interview with Beach quoted above. These facts rule out any mere misunderstanding or differing interpretation on Tripp's part; this example is typical of his inexcusable lack of scholarly accuracy. My references to his book in this and subsequent chapters are included because it stands in special need of refutation. However, there is no implication that all pro-homosexual writing is equally irresponsible.

Research on human sexual anatomy and physiology has been done only very recently, but it is of course relevant to any discussion of behavior. Modern developments in genetics and embryology have been widely misinterpreted to signify that everyone is potentially bisexual, and that homosexuality may be genetic and/or hormonal in origin. Neither of these conclusions is justified. These erroneous ideas have been used in two ways. Originally they supported the ostracism of homosexuals as essentially untreatable mistakes of nature. More recently homosexuals themselves have used these ideas to support the view that their condition is natural and therefore should not be treated.

The idea of universal human bisexual potential was introduced to modern science by Freud, from psychological evidence which has since been refuted. The motivations and psychodynamics of people who engage voluntarily in sexual relations with persons of either sex will be discussed in a later chapter. But, resting on the assumption that all people are biologically bisexual, the claim is sometimes made that the suppression of half of this potential inherent in a norm of exclusive heterosexuality in fact deprives people of a valuable social and personal asset. The highest level of adjustment, so this argument runs, would be represented neither by exclusive homosexuality or heterosexuality, but by full bisexual development for all. Do the facts about human sexual anatomy and physiology justify this point of view?

Biologically, all human and primate embryos begin as female. In those embryos having the XX chromosome pattern, a straight course of development of the reproductive system ensues which results in the birth of a female infant. Embryos having the XY chromosome pattern, however, begin very early to produce large amounts of androgen. The presence of this hormone causes a change in the original morphology of the reproductive system. Under this influence the differentiation to the male condition is completed by the third month of intrauterine life. It is true that there are small amounts of opposite sex gonadal tissue in each individual, and that this tissue produces minute amounts of the appropriate hormones. But it must be remembered that sex hormones have other functions in the body beside the regulation of specifically sexual and reproductive functions. The mere presence of both kinds is totally unrelated to any biological potential to develop into a functioning member of the opposite sex, nor does it have any causal connection with the actual sexual appetites and behavior of adults.

From time to time, there have been research reports that testosterone levels are different in male homosexuals than in heterosexuals. These studies are doubtful on technical experimental grounds; but even if future research should substantiate them, they have no bearing on the question at hand. There is no proof that the hormone level causes the behavior, only that it has been observed to occur concurrently with the behavior. It is well known that in some situations sexual activity itself affects hormone production. For example, postmenopausal women who remain sexually active continue to produce the hormones required for the maintenance of elasticity and moisture of vaginal tissue. Those who are inactive may suffer from dryness and atrophy because they stop producing the necessary hormones. In an analogous way, it is more than possible that homosexual activity itself causes the changed hormone levels which have occasionally been reported.

The evidence which has accumulated from the study of the statistically rare persons with congenital disorders is, at present, of interest and use only to specialists. It may eventually be helpful in elucidating the connections, which are not yet clear, between reproductive and sexual behavior on the one hand, and the more psychological phenomena of masculinity and feminity on the other. The widely sensationalized reports about transsexuals have been frequently used to support the view that sexual preference is innate rather than learned. While it is true that these people are untreatable by any presently known psychological techniques, there is strong evidence that their condition is the result of extremely abnormal mothering which continues the mother/child womb symbiosis and thus prevents the crucial first steps in individuation which normally take place in the first two years of life.

In conclusion, it seems clear that arguments in favor of the acceptance of homosexuality cannot be based on biological evidence, either animal or human. On the contrary, if such evidence is considered relevant at all, it points the other way.

4
Sociology and Politics

The important factors in determining any given adult's sexual behavior lie in the interaction between that person and his or her environment from birth to maturity. Temperamental constitutional predispositions play a role, but are not determinative. Clearly the attitudes and value systems of both the parents and the community will be crucial in shaping not only the growing child's behavior, but also the way that behavior is valued. For instance, a naturally quiet, unathletic boy with artistic talent will experience an entirely different acculturation process in the family of an Ivy League college professor than he will if he happens to be born into a family of coal miners. In the former, his gifts are more likely to be appreciated and his temperament respected, even if these differ from other family members. In the latter, he will probably be subjected to scorn and ridicule for being a "sissy," and as he grows older his inability and unwillingness to conform to the stereotype of competitive and aggressive behavior considered masculine in his community could (among other possibilities) contribute to an eventual homosexual adaptation.

Or, to take another example, a girl who is naturally assertive and energetic and who enjoys competitive sports will experience one sort of childhood if she is raised in an environment where marriage is considered the only desirable end for a woman and the girl's "unfeminine" traits and are seen as likely to prevent her from reaching that goal. She will experience an entirely different sort of childhood if she is surrounded by family and friends who accept and encourage her in

41

the exercise of her natural talents and who do not perceive these as detracting from her femininity or as adversely affecting her future chances of marriage. Such variations in culture and custom contribute not only to adult homosexuality but to other sexual disturbances such as frigidity, impotence or compulsive promiscuity, to name only a few.

But of course these environmental influences, significant as they are, are not enough to explain why some people suffer from difficulties in adulthood and others do not. Until the discovery by Freud of the importance of unconscious psychological processes in the formation of personality and his elaboration of psychoanalytic techniques for investigating these processes, those forms of sexual adaptation disapproved of by society, and especially (but not only) homosexuality, were viewed exclusively in moral terms. They were referred to variously as sins, vices, and forms of degeneracy, labels which to our modern ears sound more macabrely picturesque than descriptive. Freud's research convinced him otherwise, and we are indebted to him for making possible the present sophisticated understanding of the etiology of these conditions.

Because Freud failed to appreciate the fact that the psychology of women had to be considered in its own terms and not merely in some derivative relation to a male standard, his understanding of female sexuality was seriously distorted. In my opinion, this also marred his understanding of male sexuality since I do not believe that either male or female sexuality can be fully understood in isolation from the other. Our most archaic layer of basic mammalian sexual programming is, after all, directed toward the harmonious interaction of the two; even in creatures as much influenced by culture and consciousness as we humans, this is bound to have an effect, especially on the unconscious components of our behavior. Freud's formulations, therefore, were partial and inadequate by modern standards; this is no doubt why, even though he thought of homosexuality as a disturbance in development rather than merely as a peculiarly shameful kind of wickedness, he considered it essentially untreatable.

This is an important reason why psychoanalysts did not undertake the systematic study of homosexuality until about forty years ago.

Since that time an enormous amount of clinical research material has amassed and the professional literature on the subject is both extensive and thorough. Clinicians from different theoretical schools contributed to this effort, and there is a remarkable congruity in the results. At the same time, most people, including most psychiatrists, continued to view homosexuality, a condition never openly discussed and seldom even referred to in "polite society," as a weird and rare perversion. For this reason it did not engage the professional attention of most doctors. Their work was generally undertaken on those conditions which were more clearly perceived as definitely sick rather than probably wicked. But there were, fortunately, a few intrepid pioneers who took a different view and did the painstaking work of learning to understand and help homosexuals. There is a certain irony in the fact that these doctors are now under bitter attack by some homosexual activists when it is in large part due to their work that the climate of opinion changed enough to permit those activists to be heard at all!

In the next chapter I shall consider the findings of this research, but before doing so it is necessary to clear up some misunderstandings about the much publicized change in the official position of the American Psychiatric Association. Prior to 1973, homosexuality was listed in the *Diagnostic and Statistical Manual of Mental Disorders* under the main heading of "Personality Disorders and Certain Other Non-Psychotic Mental Disorders." The subheadings in this general category include "personality disorders," alcoholism, drug dependence, and sexual deviations. Homosexuality was the first of nine conditions so designated, and the others in the list were fetishism, pedophilia (preference for sexual activity with children), transvestitism, exhibitionism, voyeurism, sadism, masochism, and "other sexual deviation." The overall description of the general group of sexual deviations was as follows:

> This category is for individuals whose sexual interests are directed primarily toward objects other than people of the opposite sex, toward sexual acts not usually associated with coitus, or toward coitus performed under bizarre circumstances as in necrophilia, pedophilia, sexual sadism, and fetish-

ism. Even though many find their practices distasteful, they remain unable to substitute normal sexual behavior for them. This diagnosis is not appropriate for individuals who perform deviant sexual acts because normal sexual objects are not available to them.[1]

In the early 1970s homosexual activists staged a series of disruptive demonstrations at professional meetings, both at the local and national level. It was their claim that an important reason why their civil rights continued to be infringed upon by extremely harsh laws which subjected them to constant threat of blackmail, loss of employment and other penalties was that the medical profession insisted upon labeling them "sick." Their assertion was that there are many perfectly healthy homosexuals and that, in the absence of other pathology, there was no legitimate ground for designating sexual preference *per se* as evidence of psychiatric disorder. To do so, they said, made it impossible for them to take their rightful place as members of society equally worthy of respect and protection under the law as heterosexuals.

In December of 1973 the Board of Trustees of the American Psychiatric Association, with two-thirds of its members present, voted to change the diagnostic classification of homosexuality. It was not, as many people believe, eliminated from the *Manual,* but the description now reads differently. Instead of being called a sexual deviation it is now listed as "Sexual Orientation Disturbance" with the following qualifying paragraph:

This is for individuals whose sexual interests are directed primarily toward people of the same sex and who are either disturbed by, in conflict with, or wish to change their sexual orientation. This diagnostic category is distinguished from homosexuality, which by itself does not constitute a psychiatric disorder. Homosexuality *per se* is one form of sexual behavior, and with other forms of sexual behavior which are not by themselves psychiatric disorders, are not listed in this nomenclature.[2]

In summary, homosexuality now officially partakes of pathology only when the individual with this preference is subjectively distressed by it. The decision about whether or not it is a mental illness is thus left up to the person suffering from it. It should be obvious that this would be an extremely doubtful criterion to apply across the board to all forms of illness. Nor do there seem to have been adequate scientific reasons for making an exception in this instance. Most of the psychiatrists involved in making the decision were not specialists in homosexuality, and the extensive reports of special task forces to study it were essentially disregarded. A vigorous protest against the decision of the Board of Trustees was mounted by a group of psychiatrists who had spent their entire professional life specializing in the study and treatment of homosexuals. The eventual result of this protest was a referendum to the entire membership of the American Psychiatric Association. Shortly before the ballots were to be returned, a letter was sent out to all members by the officers of the Association, urging them not to reverse the decision of the Board of Trustees.

What did not become known until after the vote was that this letter was written and paid for by the National Gay Task Force. Over nine thousand psychiatrists (fifty-eight percent of the membership) voted in this referendum, and the Board's decision was upheld by 2,004 votes. While it is no doubt true that a number of the doctors upholding the nomenclature change had come to believe that homosexuality *per se* should not be considered an illness, it is certain that many of those voting were influenced by the letter, whose propriety was obviously questionable. Further, it is well known that psychiatrists in general are greatly concerned with issues of personal freedom and social justice. In various opinion polls their attitudes on such questions have been shown to be significantly more liberal than average; quite the reverse of physicians in general who tend to be quite conservative. Many of the voting doctors, earnestly deploring the punitive laws and harsh social treatment of homosexuals, were persuaded to vote as they did by the argument that the elimination of homosexuality as an official illness might do something to improve these regrettable conditions.

I have gone into this in some detail in order to make clear that the American Psychiatric Association decision was far from unanimous and was predominantly arrived at on socio-political rather than scientific grounds. In addition, this professional struggle illustrates the relation of science to the value system. Decisions about human behavior are never as scientific as they may look, since they are always dealing with questions of value.

In the present instance, what lies behind much of the apparently scientific discussion is really a clash between two opposing values. On the one hand, the vast majority of people in this society, including most of the psychiatrists who voted for the nomenclature change, believe that homosexuality is at least relatively abnormal. But there is another value which has emerged very strongly over the last twenty years, beginning with the struggle for black civil rights, which is that it is wrong to oppress members of minorities. Furthermore, what constitutes oppression is being defined with ever increasing subtlety. Homosexual activists have conducted their public campaigns in a rhetoric which vigorously presents them as *only* an oppressed minority. It is no accident that the bibliographies which they attach to some of their newsletters include materials about blacks and women which have no relation to the homosexual issue other than the implied association of oppressed minority status. As a result of all this, the unstated question with which many psychiatrists felt they were confronted by the activists was this: "Since I have to choose, which do I believe is more important, to uphold the idea of the abnormality of homosexuality, or to prevent the oppression of the homosexual minority?" Enough doctors chose the latter to bring about the change.

In my opinion, this shows very muddy thinking. It ought surely to be possible to consider the scientific evidence about how the homosexual adaptation is arrived at in the course of maturation as a separate issue from how homosexuals should be treated in society. This is the position taken by all responsible psychiatrists and psychologists who have devoted themselves to the investigation of homosexuality, and many of them have been in the forefront of the movement to decriminalize the condition, to put homosexual acts committed in private between consenting adults entirely beyond reach of the law.

On a different side of this question, however, are those psychiatrists who have begun to question the entire concept of mental or emotional illness. Among the most well known of these are Thomas Szasz and R. D. Laing. As always, it is difficult to do justice to the intricacies of a scholar's life work in a few sentences. With that disclaimer, their position can be loosely summarized as follows. Society has always had trouble with those whose attitudes and conduct deviate from the standards adhered to by the majority, and in various times and places different methods have been used to ostracize and punish these deviants. Currently, the most commonly used method is to declare them to be ill and, on that basis, either to incarcerate them in mental hospitals or insist that they receive treatment, the goal of which is to teach them to conform to society's standards. This system, so the argument runs, does not really tell us anything about the supposed pathology of people who are outside the usual norms, but rather reflects society's inability to tolerate eccentrics. In short, it is society that is sick, rather than the individuals society for one reason or another chooses to exclude. Some psychiatrists, persuaded by this line of reasoning, reject the evidence that homosexuality is pathological, claiming that if society accepted the behavior no pathology would ever develop in connection with it.

I believe there are serious flaws in this argument, although it is undeniable that society's treatment of many kinds of deviants has often transcended the merely uncharitable and reached the outright sadistic. But in attempting to correct these abuses I do not think it is necessary to throw the baby out with the bathwater. In learning to be more sensitive to people's right to be different, we must not lose sight of their right to be taken care of and helped when they need it. Enthusiastic proponents of the Szasz/Laing point of view do forget this and some have even urged, for instance, that it is wrong to interfere in someone's decision to commit suicide. Beyond such extreme situations, this theory rests, in general, on the assumption that there ought to be no standards of conduct beyond the one of not doing physical harm to others or depriving them of their property. Quite apart from any religious or secular moral objections to such a view, I think it ignores what is known about the nature of human community, of how people actually manage to function in groups and learn to cooperate with one another. Therefore it is quite simply unworkable.

This short description of the professional controversy now raging over homosexuality may serve to illustrate another point. Questions of what is good or bad, acceptable or unacceptable, are not decided on exclusively scientific grounds. At best, science can contribute information which can assist such decisions. Particularly true, and contrary to what many people think in this age of modern medicine, is the fact that decisions about what constitutes illness are not ultimately made on narrow scientific grounds but by the value system of the culture. Thousands of years ago Hippocrates ventured to suggest that epilepsy might be a disorder of the nervous system; he was overruled because people at that time firmly believed that it was evidence of divine possession. Neither will the final decision about homosexuality in the twentieth century be made by the medical profession. No matter how solid the scientific evidence may be for the presence or absence of pathology, it will ultimately be up to society to decide whether or not, or under what conditions, homosexual behavior will be tolerated. In the long run, it will be public opinion, not psychiatrists acting in their purely professional capacity, who will decide what appears in the *Diagnostic and Statistical Manual,* just as in the short run it was a small section of the public, homosexual activists, who forced the recent change.

5
Psychodynamics
of Male Homosexuality

Because the psychoanalytic investigation of homosexuality was begun with males, and some of the general principles which apply to both sexes were therefore discovered in that context, it will be more convenient to begin our summary of what is known about the psychodynamics by considering this material. One of the most important and truly original, ground-breaking studies was done over a ten-year period by Dr. Irving Bieber and a number of his colleagues from the Society of Medical Psychoanalysts in New York City. Preliminary results were presented to the American Psychiatric Association at its annual meeting in 1957 and the book containing the full reports was published in 1962.[1] One hundred and six male homosexuals in psychoanalysis who had sought therapy for a number of different complaints were compared with a hundred men also in therapy who were not homosexuals. As Karlen says:

> . . . the two groups closely matched in age, income, education and even in emotional problems other than homosexuality. No one has ever gathered so much finely discriminating detail on so many homosexuals, treated in depth by so many different doctors, and put through so many evaluations.[2]

What emerged from this investigation was that the family pattern of homosexuals was disturbed in characteristic ways which seldom appeared in the families of the non-homosexuals; if the disturbance was seen at all in these matched cases, it was either to a markedly lesser degree or with positive off-setting factors which were absent in the homosexual cases. This family pattern consisted of mothers who, from their sons' earliest childhood were destructively intimate by means of overprotectiveness, and by emotional and sometimes physical seductiveness. The fathers of these boys were emotionally detached from them and sometimes overtly hostile. It was clear that, of these two parental errors, the father's was determinative. As Bieber expressed it:

> We have come to the conclusion that a constructive, supportive, warmly related father *precludes* the possibility of a homosexual son; he acts as a neutralizing protective agent should the mother make seductive or close-binding attempts.[3]

Now many homosexual apologists are claiming that this theory of etiology has been disproved and discarded by all clinicians who are not "biased." This is simply untrue. In the first place, that statement of the theory is a simplified capsule summary of a considerably more complicated body of evidence, and could more accurately be said to *point to* rather than sufficiently *describe* a common etiological pattern. Secondly, no one ever claimed that this was the *only* cause of homosexuality or that it could be demonstrated in all cases.

In the fourteen years since Bieber and his colleagues published their work, and using its insights as a starting point for further clinical and research work, much has been discovered to confirm and also to amplify the original results. Dr. Lawrence Hatterer, a research clinician with more than twenty years of specialization in the field of homosexuality, says in his excellent book on the subject: "any monocular view makes a theory or therapy naive, narrow, and fatally limited."[4] He emphasizes the fact that other influences can modify or exaggerate the effect of the pattern described by the Bieber group and devotes an entire chapter to a discussion of etiological factors. These are grouped under the general headings of relationship to mother, to father, to self (search for male identity), interfamilial relationships, interpersonal relationships with non-family, and cultural and environmental influences. It is not possible to summarize this extensive material, but I refer those who are interested to Dr. Hatterer's book. Its style is easily accessible to the non-specialist, and he illustrates every point with material taken directly from taped interviews with his patients. His bibliography is an excellent guide to those who may wish to consult more technical material.

Homosexuality is not a single clinical entity. Homosexual behavior can occur under a wide variety of circumstances, with or without disturbance in gender identity, and with or without other evident dysfunctions. The homosexual act should more properly be considered a symptom, one which can occur in people who may or may not be part of a homosexual subculture. These subcultures vary considerably in style and emphasis, as well as in the particular forms of homosexual behavior which they mainly embody. Some involve massive disturbance in gender identity of members, others do not. In addition, although it is true that there are some secret homosexuals who would greatly prefer to "come out of the closet" and feel subjective relief when they manage to join openly in some aspect of homosexual life, there are many who have no desire to do so. Nor is this only because of remaining cultural sanctions against it. For some, the element of risk and thrill in leading a double life is part of their pattern. For others (many of whom are married and have children), the homosexual behavior is sporadic, occurring only in certain kinds of stress, and they themselves perceive it as problematic in terms of their primary choice of sexual orientation and lifestyle.

The many psychodynamic factors which have been found to contribute to the development of a homosexual adaptation can be conveniently summarized under three main headings: problems with unsatisfied dependency needs, problems with unresolved issues of power or dominance, and fear of heterosexuality. The first two motivations do not, at first glance, appear to be sexual, at least not in the ordinary use of that term. However, we are all familiar with the nonsexual motivations of women for engaging in genital behavior. Prostitution is an obvious example. The non-orgastic woman who does not like sex, even as an expression of intimacy, may nevertheless marry and engage in regular sexual relations for the sake of enjoying the roles of wife and mother. Those examples refer to situations in which the woman is at least partly conscious of what she is doing, but most people are also aware of the fact that loneliness and low self-esteem are frequent unconscious motivations for teen-aged girls becoming promiscuous or repeatedly pregnant.

It is less obvious, and entirely unsuspected by many, that men may also engage in genital activity for primarily nonsexual reasons. If women in this culture are often socialized to believe that they should be sexually submissive, men suffer from an equally serious complementary misapprehension, namely that unless they are sexually active, aggressive and successful there is something wrong with them. For these reasons—as well as for others of a less cultural and more personal nature—there may in both sexes be an unfortunate tendency for the necessary development of self-worth to become inappropriately contaminated by some real or imagined standard of sexual performance. This may then eventuate in genital interactions undertaken for reasons which have little if anything to do with genuine sexual attraction between compatible people. In homosexual men, this reaches an extreme in those styles of sexual contact which consist in solicitation of total strangers in such places as public toilets or steambaths. Often not a word is exchanged and the encounter may be over in a matter of minutes. Among the unconscious, primarily nonsexual reasons for engaging in this as well as other types of homosexual behavior, issues of power and dependency are commonly found. Those who find this kind of connection hard to believe are invited to consider the common aggressive expletive "Fuck you!" or the slang expression connoting defeat, "I've been screwed."

Where dependency needs are prominent, the homosexual adaptation may be resorted to in order to identify with the "masculine" strength of the partner. As one patient of mine expressed it, "it was not so much that I wanted to *love* Peter, I wanted to *be* Peter." Such men feel weak and inadequate, even though they may be in a life situation which looks successful from the outside.

Because of hostile or distant relations with a father, difficulties with a dominating mother, unresolved problems in competition with siblings or peers at various stages of growth, or some combination of these factors, issues of power may be most prominent. In this type of homosexual adaptation relationships tend to be structured in terms of dominance and submission. This is overtly displayed in some of the more pathological homosexual patterns seen in men's prisons where the "pecking order" among the inmates may be established in terms of who must submit to whose sexual advances. It is not uncommon for homosexual rape to occur under these conditions. However, the same dynamics may surface during analysis of perfectly civilized men in more normal circumstances. A patient of mine whose behavior at his very responsible job was always calm and deferential, had a boss with an extremely volatile temper which was frequently vented in outbursts of anger at subordinates. After some months of therapy my patient noticed that his periodic need for a homosexual encounter with some man socially inferior to himself, an encounter during which he regularly took the aggressive role, always followed occasions when he had been the target of one of his employer's tirades.

When fear of heterosexuality is prominent in the psychodynamics, its effects may be seen in different forms and to varying degrees. In many cases the homosexual man may enjoy good relationships, sometimes even close friendships, with women; here the fear is confined to the sphere of overt sexual encounter, and may not be consciously perceived even as aversion. Such a man may say, "I get along fine with women—only for some reason they just don't turn me on." In the course of therapy, in such cases usually undertaken for some symptom unrelated to the homosexual adaptation, it is not uncommon to discover extremely odd circumstances relating to the patient's mother. These may even include such things as her insistence upon supervising his baths as late as age twelve or thirteen, down to such details as making sure he has washed his genitals properly! But even for less obvious reasons, some problem related to the Oedipal conflict is almost sure to emerge. Other homosexual men may be much more aware of their problems with women, which may range from mild or occasional discomfort through severe and consistent hostility. Men with these extreme manifestations usually withdraw into one of the homosexual subcultures which preclude all social contacts with women, though some may be able to associate with lesbians. In addition to faulty resolution of the childhood Oedipal stage, such conditions may arise from patterns of child-rearing which are excessively harsh on the one hand or extremely overprotective on the other, thus inhibiting the development of the capacity for adequate self-assertion. Since in this culture assertiveness is usually seen as an indispensable component of masculinity, such influences may interfere with appropriate sexual identity, and one of the homosexual adaptive styles may be a solution to the difficulty. Usually there are elements of all three of these main psychodynamic categories in committed homosexuals, and they occur in varying proportions.

Highly competitive societies tend to produce a greater number of homosexuals than do less competitive ones; it is therefore predictable that the dependency or power motivations may be prominent in such cases. Obvious effeminacy is not very common. When it occurs, its psychological function seems to be an avoidance of any appearance of aggressiveness. As Karlen says:

> . . . effeminacy seems to be a misleadingly named body language that combines reversal of masculine signals, non-assertive signs, and some elements of burlesqued feminity to announce "I won't fight, I'm not dangerous—if necessary, not even a man."[5]

At the other end of the scale, it is not uncommon for episodic homosexuality in an otherwise heterosexual man to appear precisely in situations of competitive stress at the job or elsewhere.

Perhaps the best illustration of some of these motivations is to be found in the writing of C. A. Tripp, already referred to in Chapter Three. Presumably he intends to describe "normal, well-adjusted" homosexuals, but I will let readers judge for themselves. First, some sample comments about heterosexuality:

Besides the strains inherent in making close emotional contacts with the opposite sex, there are dangers in overcloseness: To really understand a woman and be understood by her, a man often feels he has to make serious compromises in his general posture.

Are these strains not acquired rather than inherent?

Why would a man feel compromised by this, unless he believes women make demands which assault his identity as a man, and which he is powerless to resist?

To give up more than a fraction of his autonomy and to move in the direction of softness may strike him as a watering down of the purified maleness he has gone to some trouble attaining.

Many men stifle these risks at the outset by holding on to a certain coarseness and avoiding all delicately intimate contacts with women.

Other men solve the problem by going ahead with a very close contact ... but then returning immediately to their male friends with whom they rejuvenate their male outlook. Thus a major continuing motivation for the male bond is apparent: It is the ballpark (sometimes literally) in which a somewhat bent masculinity is bolstered and restored to its original shape.[6]

. . . there is also much in people which makes them want to hold on to the undiluted purity of their hard-won gender eccentricity. Men especially are inclined to want to keep their one-sidedness, their distinctively male outlook, come what may.[7]

Sexual zest does not arise from the comforts of similarity and agreement . . . sexual attraction requires the sharper zap of clash or foreignness—a note of antagonism set in a disparity of outlook or of rank. Consequently, a certain enmity between the sexes, be it expressed in the downing of women or in the nearly universal battle-of-the-sexes, has always been central to their attraction.[8]

Is there no interaction between equals? Even if women are "soft," can he see no way of relating to them other than by identifying with them? Why was it so hard to learn to be a man?

Is true masculinity really characterized by coarseness?
Delicately? Are women frail underneath that demanding assaultiveness on his manhood?

Are women really vampires draining a man inevitably of his male outlook? Does associating with other men give a "masculinity transfusion"? Are male friendships really based on a defense against being "feminized"?

One hardly has to be a Freudian to see castration anxiety in this image.

Just what is it in people which makes them want to do this?
Could it be unconscious pathology which causes them to see the other sex as carriers of "impurity"?
Or to experience their own sexual identity as so shaky they have to go out of their way to "hold on to" it?

This would come as a surprise to marriage counselors.

Do people get divorced because they get along too well?

For Tripp, the dominance/submission axis seems more prominent than issues of dependency, as evidenced by the following quotations:

Sexual attraction thrives when and only when the partners are in some sense alienated from each other.[9]

. . . all sexual attractions depend upon resistance barriers and . . . a man's attraction to a partner (and thus his arousability) is almost invariably keyed into dominant and not to democratic motifs.[10]

Does he only know about diluted rape?

Has he never heard of devoted rapture?

. . . all sexual attractions are based on positive motives: the real or imagined benefits a person hopes to gain by a sexual conquest or by "possessing" a partner.[11]

How can you possess a partner?

Isn't that a contradiction in terms? Are other people only to be used?

. . . there is no difference between the origin of homosexuality in the case of the "champion" and in that of the frail fellow with the inferiority feelings. In both cases, male attributes have become eroticized through extreme admiration of them.[12]

Does extreme admiration always get eroticized?
Exactly why is it eroticized in these cases?

Tripp uses the word "inversion" to mean *any* departure from the extreme stereotype of "primal-scene sex," male aggresive-intrusive, female passive-submissive. As originally used by psychiatrists, inversion is actually confined to consistent disturbance in some aspect of sexual identification, but Tripp uses it indiscriminately. This is evidently in the service of guarding his "hard-won masculinity" which he defines in bizarrely narrow terms, and clearly supports by aggressive character defenses:

Inversion . . . a basic capacity for behavioral reversal that pervades not only sex, but religion and philosophy as well. . . . Momentary inversions (including those that last for the duration of a sexual contact) are so much a part of both heterosexual and homosexual relations as to be taken as a matter of course. . . . At the other extreme, it is tempting to rate as super-irregular all those extraordinary ongoing inversions, be they effeminacy, transsexuality, loving thine enemy, or any constant application of the Christian ethic.[13]

What kind of a man perceives the ability to give unselfishly, or to forgive others as a "super-irregular" lapse from true masculinity?

Not surprisingly, he goes on to describe his own therapeutic technique with homosexuals who come to him for help with other problems in the following words:

Any therapist who fully accepts a person's basic sexual orientation has an enormous advantage; he can do what no change-therapist could ever get away with: He can zero in on particular trouble spots with a kind of flagrant brutality (actually, an affectionate abuse) . . .[14]

This passage is describing his approach to men who suffer from the effeminate gestures and behavior discussed above. Apparently Tripp sees no inconsistency in finding that pathological, since it conflicts with his horrifying concept of true masculinity. It seems to me that in the course of his attempt to deny the validity of the classic psychiatric theories of homosexuality, Tripp himself demonstrates them in almost pure form.

Where these basic disturbances of maturation exist—infantile dependency needs expressed either directly or by compensation, inappropriate concern with dominance/submission issues, and fear of heterosexuality—they do not always express themselves in either a partial or complete homosexual adaptation. Those who are familiar with the first three stages of psychosexual development as outlined by Freud will know that infantile dependency needs are primarily related to problems in the oral phase, dominance/submission issues to the anal phase, and fear/hostility in relation to the opposite sex to the Oedipal phase. This is a great oversimplification, since there can be input from each stage to issues which are more basically related to another stage. In addition, regression to a more or less successfully negotiated earlier stage may occur if problems arise later. The entire development of the personality is usually not affected, but only parts; and specific interactions with significant relatives and friends, with the environment, and with the general atmosphere of the culture all play a part. There is a sense in which *every* neurosis can be described as relating to one or more of these issues. In fact, one of the still unsolved puzzles is what Freud referred to as the "choice of neurosis." People of essentially similar backgrounds, even siblings raised in the same traumatic family, may show widely divergent solutions to the conflicts which their growth involves. One may even turn out "perfectly normal," while the others may choose different neurotic solutions. Nor is there any sure way to predict degree of impairment of function or of subjective discomfort in individual cases. Statistically one may know that from such and such a background this or that neurosis is more likely to develop, or is very rare, but a particular case is always in some sense mysterious.

These points are emphasized to show the unscientific and illogical nature of one kind of argument commonly used by homosexual apologists. They claim that because it cannot be demonstrated that X factor *always* causes homosexuality, or because *all* homosexuals do not suffer from X factor, then there can be no relation between X and homosexuality. But the same kind of statements can be made about *every* psychological impairment, and about most physical ones as well. For example, psychiatric treatment of persons suffering from hypertension usually reveals repressed anger, and when this is dealt with successfully in psychotherapy the hypertension may be relieved. This is true often enough to be useful, but is not true in all cases, and even where the anger is demonstrable, cure is not always possible. Someone bent on proving that anger or hypertension is "normal" might, however, try to attack the empirical facts in the manner described.

Nevertheless, the origins of homosexuality (or of any other dysfunction) are not sealed in the first six years of life, important as those years are. Experiences throughout the latency period between age six or seven and the onset of puberty are also important. It was originally thought that this period was one in which psychosexual development was essentially dormant, the growth process being focused on other tasks. Subsequent research has shown this not to be the case. Particularly important during this time are the development of satisfactory peer relationships and experiences of competitiveness, aggressiveness, success, or failure.

It is the internal and external experiences of adolescence which are probably decisive in most cases. For those whose family life has been fraught with extremes of those factors which have been found to predispose boys to the development of adult homosexuality, it would take an exceptionally fortunate set of circumstances in adolescence to avert that outcome. For instance, it sometimes happens that the troubled parents who are acting out their difficulties in the pathological ways described above may seek help for themselves. As a result of therapy they may realize what they have been doing to their son and be able to reverse the process. Or a boy may be sent to live with healthy relatives or to a good coeducational boarding school away from the pernicious influences which have distorted his development up to that point.

Even in the most favorable family environments, adolescence is a very troublesome and chaotic period of rapid development along all fronts during which boys go through a period of what is usually called "sexual identity confusion." This does not necessarily mean that they are uncertain about their gender identification, though some may be, due to early problems. They may be perfectly sure that they are, and want to be, members of their own sex in every sense. What it does mean is that they do not yet know *how* to be adult males, and without this knowledge it is extremely difficult to know *how* to approach girls. It is for this reason that they characteristically go through a period of associating principally, if not exclusively, with other boys. This period is often referred to as the "normal homosexual phase." Again, this is a misleading label, even though some "homosexual" acting out such as group masturbation is common. Actually, it would be more accurate in most cases to think of these boys as testing their equipment. If one compares this description of adolescence with the remarks quoted above from Tripp, it can be seen that he simply assumes that these adolescent attitudes are continued into chronological maturity as a matter of course.

Adolescent boys often worry about whether they are "queer." This involves concern about whether they are "masculine" enough, however they and their community define that term. Even in some subcultures where gangs of teen-aged boys regularly engage in homosexual prostitution to get extra money, as long as they retain the sexual role of inserter they do not consider themselves to be homosexual—their own sense of their gender identity is not impaired.[15] Usually, even from such backgrounds, they turn to exclusive heterosexuality upon reaching maturity. But of course homosexual acts engaged in during this adolescent stage may trigger unresolved difficulties from earlier stages and may precipitate a more serious or lasting homosexual commitment.

Our culture is extremely competitive and power-oriented, sometimes in crassly materialistic or aggressive terms which are clearly identifiable as offensive; but often this takes place in more subtle ways, such as the liberal, educated family's insistence on the "pursuit of excellence." This kind of pressure on the already beleaguered male adolescent may precipitate at least transitory homosexual adaptation for the reasons cited in the discussion of dependency and dominance issues. Because cultural expectations and pressures play a very significant part in the shaping of adolescent identity, it is easy to see that if a youngster is in any way torn by such problems, it may make a difference if he is surrounded by a climate of opinion which rejects homosexuality as an acceptable life style, rather than by one which tells him that homosexuality is not only acceptable but probably normal. If he is the idealistic type who is drawn to champion underdogs and victims, this may give further impetus to him to opt for the homosexual stopping place, given the present tenor of much homosexual rhetoric.

The crucial fact is that, while homosexual behavior may be only experimental in adolescence, it can all too easily become a fixed pattern because of the great importance of learning, experience, and habituation in the development of human sexuality. Many men come for treatment who regret having made the homosexual choice at an age when they were too immature to understand its full implications.

There is a final ironic twist, illustrating the perennial capacity of adolescents to be at least one unexpected and frightening jump ahead of their elders. A recent report reveals that in a discussion group of adolescents who identified themselves as homosexuals, five of the eight core members turned out not to be homosexual at all! Why was such a claim ever made, since this group was entirely voluntary? The author of the report says:

> Declaring oneself a homosexual may be a way of seeking independence from his family rather than an expression of true sexual preference. . . . Identification with homosexuality, an anathema to most parents, may not only provide a supportive frame-work, but may also abruptly hasten the separation process through parental withdrawal, giving the adolescent an increased sense of independence and maturity.[16]

Is any further proof required of the transitory nature and uncertain significance of youthful sexual expression? While it is true that a small number of males who become committed homosexuals in adult life have consciously experienced this as an overpowering inclination from an early age, such cases constitute a small minority. It is unscientific as well as unethical to consider homosexuality as a settled diagnosis for anyone under the age of at least twenty-one.

Naturally this does not mean that boys or young men who seek advice or help, giving homosexual acts or fantasies as their reason for requesting the consultation, should be told to go away and stop worrying. Anyone seeking help for any reason, should always be taken seriously. Nevertheless, it is important for counselors of any background, religious or psychological, to have a firm grasp of the distinction between taking people's complaints *seriously* and taking them *literally.*

6
Male and
Female Sexuality Compared

*T*he discussion of female homosexuality will necessarily be less conclusive and more speculative than that of male homosexuality. Scanty as our knowledge of human sexuality is—compared, say, with what is known about such scientific subjects as the structure of the atom, liver function in rats, or metallurgy—we know even less about women than we do about men. The historical aspects of this ignorance were discussed in Chapter Two. But there are other reasons why lesbians have been less visible than their male counterparts.

For some 150 years Anglo-Saxon culture has been extremely intolerant of any physical manifestation of friendship between men. Any public display of emotion, other than anger, indignation, or moderate expression of aggressive and competitive feeling, has been thought to signify an unmanly degree of irrationality or loss of control. This has been far less true in the Latin countries of both hemispheres, where men may walk down the street arm in arm and the ceremonial embrace is part of the accepted etiquette of formal occasions. In England and the United States, on the other hand, such behavior was considered at least effeminate, if not actually homosexual, and it was not uncommon for very young boys (at least of the upper and middle classes) to be taught that shaking hands was the only acceptable way to greet another male, even their own fathers and brothers! Paradoxically (at least to the female mind) a much lower standard of modesty has prevailed between men than between women. Men customarily have gone swimming together in the nude and their locker rooms and lavatories offer no privacy. Fortunately the bizarrely artificial prohibitions against showing perfectly normal human feelings have relaxed considerably in the last ten years; physical gestures of friendship between men are no longer perceived as necessarily sexual or even in poor taste, except by those who are morbidly conventional.

Women have never been bound by such peculiar structures. Displays of emotion have always been assumed to be integral to their sex and female relatives and friends may customarily greet one another with a kiss no matter how recent their last encounter. At the same time, there has been a consistent standard of physical modesty for women. Public facilities of all kinds provide privacy for women and, until very recently, it was rare for women to disrobe completely in one another's presence.

Such social customs would obviously make any sexual overtures or behavior between men relatively conspicuous, while similar interactions between women might well go unnoticed. If it is remembered that until about fifteen years ago the subject of homosexuality was simply not discussable and was practically never referred to directly in print outside of professional journals and pornography, it will be easier to understand why many people, particularly women, had never even heard of it. Most of those who were aware of it had only the vaguest idea of what it entailed and would never have imagined that such a condition could possibly affect anyone they knew. At that time, it was widely assumed by the general public that all male homosexuals were obviously effeminate. It was further assumed that lesbians would be identifiably masculine in deportment and dress. Even here it would have been necessary to go quite far to arouse the average person's suspicion, especially when it was still a high compliment to tell a woman "You think like a man!" and imitation of men was easily dismissed as evidence of mere jealousy of their privilege.

Beyond these cultural reasons for the relative invisibility of lesbians, there are more serious academic reasons why less is known about them. These are related to the development of psychoanalytic theory over the course of the last seventy-five years. Before going on to discuss what *is* known about the psychodynamics of homosexuality in women, it will be necessary to talk about female sexuality in more general terms, and to describe how it differs in principle from male sexuality.

It is fashionable in some circles to be harshly critical of Freud and to blame him for what is perceived as the contemporary exacerbation of the oppression of women. Particularly under attack are his theories of penis envy, narcissism and shame, which he felt were universal in women. He even believed that motherhood was linked to female inferiority since a baby could compensate, only partially to be sure, for the absent penis! But no genius, not even Freud, can entirely transcend the intellectual and social preconceptions of their time. He did not realize that women brought up in a culture which prized male attributes and considered feminine traits valuable mainly to the extent that they provided reproductive and social support for men's activities, might well experience various kinds of inferiority feelings on this account.

The great advantage which the theories of Carl Jung have over those of Sigmund Freud is that they accord to the feminine principle full autonomy and equality, and acknowledge that the feminine must be understood in its own terms rather than in some derivative relation to the masculine. For him and his followers the human psyche is fundamentally androgynous. Those qualities which are included in the "feminine principle" manifest consciously in women, but through the unconscious in men where they are referred to as the *anima*. The "masculine principle" manifests consciously in men, but in women it is expressed through the unconscious as *animus*. The whole problem of sex role stereotyping which has plagued us for so long arises from the tendency not to integrate that which is unconscious, but to project it onto persons of the other sex. The tendency to project rather than to integrate is of course not confined to this issue. It forms the backbone of the dynamics of paranoia where it is carried to an extreme— the sufferers, unable to acknowledge their own negative thoughts or feelings, and with an ego insufficiently developed to permit successful repression, experience them as though they were originating outside their own psyche, and this results in the familiar delusions of persecution. In a non-psychotic form this dynamic is also expressed in the New Testament admonition to remove the beam from your own eye before you take the mote out of your brother's.

The differences between masculine and feminine psychology are not postulated as differences in content so much as in style, degree of consciousness, emphasis, proportion, and order of priority naturally assigned to things. In a commendable effort to help the culture rid itself of the old sexual stereotypes, many have claimed that there really is no difference between men and women which is not the result of the socialization process. But this has unwittingly included the assumption that the traditional feminine roles and attributes are inferior while those of men are superior. Thus the declaration of equality without a difference too often turns into the very destructive attempt on the part of women to assume masculine values and sometimes even to denigrate the feminine. In short, without realizing it they take up the very cudgels they are urging men to put down. This is peculiarly unfortunate since Western culture is suffering from a runaway development of the masculine principle and is sadly lacking an equally sophisticated elaboration of the feminine.

The delineation of precisely what the difference between masculine and feminine is cannot be adequately undertaken here for reasons of space. Those wishing to read more at first hand are invited to consult the references given in the notes for this chapter.[1] But perhaps an analogy may serve to give a rough idea. Consider the human eye. We have two types of vision, macular and peripheral. The first is what we use when we wish to focus on something, to be able to see details with precision. Peripheral vision gives us the larger context in which the object we are scrutinizing is situated. In addition, peripheral vision is more sensitive to faint light sources than is macular vision. We have all had the experience of seeing a star out of the corner of our eye, only to have it disappear when we attempt to look straight at it. But without that faint, indirect glimpse we would not know where to direct our telescope. Only a fool would claim that one kind of vision is better than the other, since both are truly essential to the faculty of sight. Without the context we would not be able to know what we are looking at. Without the focus we would not be able to see anything clearly. In this analogy, the masculine principle corresponds to focused vision, and the feminine to peripheral. As Jung himself expresses it, *"Perfection* is a masculine desideratum, while woman inclines by nature to *completeness."*[2]

What this translates into in terms of human behavior is that men on the whole *tend* to be task- or performance-oriented and consider problems analytically, while women *tend* to be relationship-oriented and deal with situations in their entirety, or synthetically. It cannot be too strongly stressed that this does not mean that women cannot, given sufficient motivation and encouragement, perform just as well as men. Nor does it mean that men, again given sufficient motivation and encouragement, cannot be just as competent as women in dealing with relationships, or in keeping track of the total context of problems. In the heyday of sexual stereotyping, of course, the motivation and encouragement for both men and women to use these alternate faculties consciously and effectively has often been absent. The current women's movement rhetoric stresses the ways in which women's development has been stunted, but of course the same thing is true of men.

In my opinion, the lot of men has been even worse in some ways, since they know far less about women than women do about men. Since the educational system was originally designed by and for men, it has traditionally fostered the development of masculine values; this tendency becomes increasingly pronounced the higher the level, reaching its peak in graduate schools. This means that any woman in the course of acquiring an education has been obliged to bring her own unconscious contrasexual component (her *animus*) into some degree of function. It is also because of their subsidiary position during the millennia of the patriarchal system that women have had to know much about men. Since men were always officially in charge, they could successfully project whatever they wished onto women, whereas women, in order to survive, always had to be somewhat more practical. Traditional feminine "deviousness" in managing men, often ruthlessly successful, testifies to this. On the other hand it is possible for a man to go through his whole life without ever dealing with his own contrasexual component (his *anima*) except unconsciously or by getting the women around him to carry his projections of it. Fortunately, few have gone this far. Just how ingrained these techniques are can be seen from the fact that Freud himself, who worked extremely hard at trying to understand, late in life confessed that he had never been able to figure out what women really want. That this difficulty was aggravated if not caused by his never questioning their fundamentally subsidiary role is revealed by a proud comment he made about his only daughter, who became a famous psychoanalyst in her own right and far outstripped her brothers in fame and performance: "Anna is my only son!"

It was not until the last ten years or so that classical Freudian psychoanalytic theories about female psychology were brought into serious question. Until very recently, the Jungian theories had not received wide attention; almost no organized research has been undertaken from that point of view. It is for these theoretical reasons that any discussion of any aspect of female sexuality is bound to be less comprehensive and less accurate than one might wish. The tendency to take what is known about men and attempt to transpose it to women, often bending or ignoring the evidence in order to make the theories fit, is all too widespread. What is needed is for clinicians and research workers to take a fresh look at women, as though they had never even heard of men.

The bizarre controversy about the nature of female orgasm is a case in point. This began with Freud, who took the view that clitoral orgasm was immature and that a woman who had overcome all of her neurotic difficulties in accepting her feminine role would experience only vaginal orgasm. The effects of this odd patriarchal idea on women patients, giving them yet one more thing to feel inferior about, are by now well known. While Masters and Johnson are to be commended for beginning modern research on human sexual phsysiology, their work should have been understood as a tentative starting point in a new field rather than as the last word on the subject. They have made a number of errors, not least among which is to confuse sexual physiology with sexuality itself. It is their view that all female orgasms are clitoral, and this "discovery" has been widely hailed. Heterosexual women whose own experience is limited to this type of orgasm are glad to be exonerated from imputations of immaturity or neurosis. Psychotherapists are relieved of the protracted task, so frequently unsuccessful, of getting their women patients to graduate to "mature" vaginal orgasm. Lesbians have also welcomed this view, since it relieves them of the suspicion that they may be missing something enjoyed by heterosexual women and confirms their belief that men are superfluous, except as agents of impregnation. (As we shall see later, this conscious belief does not withstand the intense scrutiny of psychoanalytic investigation.)

The very obvious solution which few writers on the subject seem to have thought of is that women have more than one kind of orgasm. It is especially odd that this possibility has received so little attention since it has been known for a long time that women have more diffuse sexual responses and more erogenous zones than men. Of course this too has been attributed by some to women being more "primitive" than men. Focus has been valued more highly than context not only psychologically, but physically as well. The underlying assumption seems clearly to have been that since the male orgasm physiologically occurs in one place and at a definite time, the female orgasm must be similar.

Two writers who know better, however, are Alex Comfort and Irving Singer. Dr. Comfort's famous book, *The Joy of Sex,* just takes for granted that women have an especially wide variety of orgasmic possibilities; he stresses that any claims of superiority of one form over another are simply fatuous.[3] Since he addresses himself to sexual subtleties far more delicate than anything Masters and Johnson could possibly elicit from couples performing under klieg lights and before television cameras, he also does not confuse ejaculation with orgasm for the male, but recognizes that the subjective experience of the same physiological response may vary much more than is usually suspected.

The very best writer I have found on this subject is Irving Singer, a professor of philosophy at the Massachusetts Institute of Technology. His truly illuminating book, *The Goals of Human Sexuality,* contains an excellent criticism of Masters and Johnson; he is precise and acute in finding the logical flaws in the work of numerous other researchers and theorists in the field of sexology.[4] His discussion and description are beautifully nuanced and include detailed accounts by women of their total sexual response. The physical reactions are described not in isolation but in the psychological and emotional context in which they actually occur. This results in the only reports I have ever read which I felt were an accurate reflection of feminine sexual experience as I have come to know it over the years of my psychiatric practice, as well as from descriptions by women who are not in therapy. He prefers a different terminology to the customary distinction between clitoral and vaginal. Instead, he speaks of vulval, uterine, and blended, which is the relatively rare occurrence of the first two simultaneously. The uterine type is the result of rhythmic pressure on internal organs, and by its very nature is not susceptible to the kind of technical investigation which can yield information about orgasms originating on the surface of the body. In the present state of research techniques, subjective reports must be relied upon. The common scientific error of declaring nonexistent or trivial those phenomena which one is unable to measure is particularly distorting in this instance.

I do not, however, think it would be altogether fair to *blame* the preponderantly male clinical and research establishment for this sorry state of the art of understanding female sexuality. In the first place, some women really do suffer from such things as penis envy. More than once in my professional career I have toyed with the idea of giving up that concept altogether only to have some woman come into my office and in the very first interview tell me that as a child she desperately wanted to be a boy and the worst frustration of her life was when she finally had to accept the fact that she could not urinate standing up! I have also seen women who really did have the fantasy that their babies were substitutes for the missing penis. Naturally they make dreadful mothers. At the present time we can only speculate about how frequent such cases would be in a culture which valued women appropriately and on their own terms.

Second, and much more important, is the fact that men and women really do have very different ways of approaching sex. Naturally the research workers and clinicians themselves, whether male or female, are not exempt. Unless they are aware of the difference, problems in research design, reporting and interpretation of results are likely to ensue.

There used to be an old proverb which stated that men give love to get sex, whereas women give sex to get love. Put thus baldly, it is of course not true, but it does point in the right direction. Particularly in adolescence and young adulthood, before the maturation process has progressed far enough for the unconscious contrasexual component (*animus* or *anima,* as the case may be) to be much recognized and integrated, there is a strong tendency for men to be primarily interested in the physical aspects of sex while women tend to be primarily interested in the social and emotional concomitants of it. This is probably biologically programmed to some extent, and had obvious evolutionary advantages in the earlier eras of human development. For at least one sex to be strongly motivated at the physical level had clear reproductive value for a struggling species. As we shall see, women are strongly inclined to put sex in a relationship context, and this too would provide an evolutionary advantage in terms of favoring social development. We do know that on the average men respond very easily to visual cues for sexual arousal in a way that women generally do not. Young men hanging out on the street corner engaged in girl watching are fantasizing about which girl they might like to go to bed with, and the mere sight of a pretty girl can produce an erection. Furthermore, they are often not aroused by the whole girl, but narrow their attention to a particular anatomical feature. Years ago, before the consciousness raising activities of the women's liberation movement made such frankness unlikely if not impossible, some of my male classmates as late as medical school used to describe themselves as "leg men" or "tit men." As I recall, the women in the class found this highly amusing. I have found that the more mature (as distinguished from merely older) men get, the less likely they are to persist in these essentially adolescent patterns of female evaluation. Still, young women who insist on dressing provocatively in such garb as miniskirts or no bra on a Junoesque figure, but also feel free to be indignant when their appearance is the subject of coarse comment by passing men, are simply ignoring a basic biological fact of male sexual patterning. Less politely put, they are cockteasers. I do not deny that mannerly men will probably refrain from such remarks even when sorely provoked, but their thoughts are straying just the same.

Beyond this visual arousability pattern, there are other noteworthy origins of the characteristic male emphasis on the physical aspects of sex. No boy ever goes through puberty without becoming specifically and acutely aware of his sexual drives, regardless of what attitudes to sex have been conveyed to him through his upbringing. The spontaneous erection and the wet dream are universal male experiences and these may (and usually do) occur entirely outside of the context of any personal relationship, whether heterosexual or homosexual. A boys' need is *first* experienced as purely physical, and it is only through the socialization process that he gradually learns to coordinate this need with the other values and requirements of life. Some men unfortunately do not get past the state of seeing their sexuality as a weapon in competitive or aggressive situations. The quotes from Tripp in the last chapter are a good illustration of this. Most men eventually learn to integrate it with more civilized and unitive feelings. Still, it is not uncommon for a man's sexual urges (as distinct from his sexual commitments, if any) to remain more or less independent of his relationships, nor does this fact mean that there is necessarily anything wrong with him.

A classic example of this is the familiar marital situation in which after a day of disharmony or actual fighting the husband may without any conciliatory preamble make sexual overtures to his wife. Not uncommonly, she responds with a fresh round of hurt or indignation: "How can you think of such a thing! You haven't said a civil word to me all day, never mind a loving one!" That scene can be played with many different endings, but it could be avoided altogether if she understood that such behavior is perfectly natural to him and does not necessarily mean that he thinks of her only as a sexual convenience. He, on the other hand, would do well to remember that sexual interest is far more likely for her than it is for him to be inextricably linked to the overall state of their relationship at a given time.

Even in the most sexually "liberated" society puberty affects girls quite differently. Menstruation and breast development are explained and experienced as preparations for the possibility of motherhood, not as occasions of inescapable sexual arousal. What girls experience *first* in the sexual sphere is the wish for friendships with boys. If they are socialized in a milieu which is sexually permissive, they will conclude that the way to form these desired relationships is to be sexually available, and they will behave accordingly. If, as in former times and other places, they are raised in an atmosphere which suggests that the best way to relate to boys is to be sexually unavailable, then that is what they will do. The recognition of their own specifically sexual needs and responses generally has to be learned in either case. Nature does not force these lessons on them in any obvious way as it does for their brothers. Some girls discover the art of masturbation accidentally, but many more must be taught. Many never discover it at all. Before the sexual information explosion of the twenty years since the Kinsey report, it was not uncommon even for married orgastic women to be so unaware of their own anatomy that they did not know about the existence of the clitoris, let alone its role in the sexual pleasure they so regularly enjoyed. As was long suspected and conclusively demonstrated by Kinsey, it is rare for women to reach orgasm during intercourse until they have been sexually active for some time, often years, and this can be entirely unrelated to the question of whether they find sex enjoyable. In general, they reach the peak of their sexual responsiveness in their thirties or even later, many women reporting their first orgasms after menopause. Since the so-called sexual liberation, women know more about the anatomy and techniques of sex than formerly, and they tend to begin their sexual experience at a younger age. According to the 1975 *Redbook* Report," which analyzed questionnaires returned by over one hundred thousand women (making it the largest single sample ever taken on any aspect of sexuality, male or female) ninety percent of married women under age twenty-five have had pre-marital intercourse.[5] At the time of the Kinsey report this figure was only thirty-three percent. But the basic pattern of later flowering of full appreciation and enjoyment of sexual experience for women than for men persists.

Women never lose the preference for sexual encounters occurring in the context of an otherwise satisfying ongoing relationship. This is not merely a preference, it is an actual need. I have both treated and known socially many young women in the last ten years who have done their valiant misguided best to live up to the "liberated" idea that it is not only permissible but is even desirable to be sexually compliant with men whom they know so slightly that there has been no opportunity to form a relationship with any substance on the emotional, mental or spiritual planes. Without exception, they have sooner or later rejected this pattern, recognizing that it leads at least to unhappiness if not to actual neurosis. Some of the more ardent feminists have felt guilty about this decision, seeing it as ideological backsliding, as a failure to claim their "sexual rights" on an equal footing with men. But those who do not confuse the concept of equality with the notion that men and women are alike, perceive it as a step forward in which they claim their specifically feminine rights, including the unquestioned right to say no when they feel like it. Furthermore, just as a man is not obliged to explain and justify logically his wish for a sexual encounter, so a woman should not be obliged to explain or justify her wish *not* to have one. *That* is equality. Naturally, there are situations in which these roles are reversed, but they are less common and tend to give less trouble when they do occur. Unlike a woman, when a man doesn't want to, he usually can't. While it is true that sexually experienced women learn to identify their physical urges as such, these are likely to remain much more diffuse and more easily divertible into other channels than is the case for men. This does *not* mean that their sexual urges are weaker than men's, and in particular cases the reverse is often true; it only means that they are different. *Consistent* (as opposed to occasional) detachment of these sexual impulses from women's emotions and from their attitudes to their partners is extremely rare if it even occurs at all in the absence of psychopathology.

The way in which these differences may affect research and its interpretation can also be demonstrated. One of the most vociferous critics of Masters and Johnson is a woman psychiatrist in New York, Dr. Natalie Shainess. Her objections all center around the detachment of the physical sexual experience from the total context of the relationship between partners, and she cites the use of female sexual surrogates as especially degrading. Objecting to Masters and Johnson's statement that "Regardless of the individual problems, most participants who complete . . . [the clinic's course] . . . can overcome them" she replies that "what is much more likely is that couples having a poor sex relationship do not love each other in a true sense, and there are likely to be serious problems—of an interpsychological and interpersonal nature—between the partners." Unlike Masters and Johnson, she does not view infidelity as a sexual problem, but as an interpersonal one. In an article written to defend Masters and Johnson against Dr. Shainess' attack, Dr. Judd Marmor, a past president of the American Psychiatric Association with many years of clinical and research experience in the sexual field, accuses her of "prudish resistance and hostility." He excuses Masters and Johnson's failure to fully investigate the psychological dimensions of sex on the grounds that funds to do so were unavailable, without appearing to realize that in her view this omission makes their results almost worthless. He dismisses her insistence on the need for a creative love relationship in the following words: "It is precisely this kind of sentimental mystique about sexuality that lies behind so many problems of sexual inadequacy."[6]

To me the most interesting thing about this exchange is that Dr. Shainess is clearly exhibiting the typical feminine approach to sex as I described it earlier, while Dr. Marmor is equally clearly showing the more masculine focus on the physical aspects, without being able to appreciate the fact that the larger context she attempts to provide is essential to good sexual relationships. Most mature men (in Jungian terms, this would include being in good touch with the *anima*) do better than this. Kenneth Keniston, for instance, as well as Irving Singer, both understand Dr. Shainess' view much better than Marmor appears to.[7] Of course women who are not well related to their *animus* often fail to get connected with the primarily physical aspects of their sexuality, and this may result in frigidity and prudishness or in compulsive, joyless promiscuity.

This difference between the male and female viewpoints can be equally well illustrated from less conventional sources. In the summer of 1973 I had a long interview with Margo St. James, the San Francisco madam who has been attempting to organize prostitutes in order to decriminalize the profession and to help the women in it operate independently of all those individuals and groups who presently exploit them. To my intense surprise I discovered that she and I were in essential agreement about the nature of sex and its role in human affairs, although we parted company on the question of how best to deal with the present problems. At the root of the difficulties, she felt, was the divorce between sex and emotion, but she saw women themselves as fostering this. By far the majority of her customers are married men, and she blamed their wives for using sex as a weapon instead of integrating it into the total fabric of the relationship. She saw herself and her co-workers as performing a necessary ministry to men whose wives did not understand and implement their feminity appropriately, and who had no idea of the real nature of male sexuality. She saw the devalued role of women in this culture as contributing both to the failures of the wives and to the exploitation of prostitutes. If things were as they should be, she thought, neither her profession nor mine would be necessary. (With that statement I could heartily agree!)

Contrast this essentially feminine view with these comments by C. A. Tripp which constitute an extremely low-level exaggeration of the more typically male approach:

> On close examination, nearly every adult's highest level of response is limited to particular kinds of partners, and to relatively few situations that

fulfill specific personal demands—demands that are highly fetishlike in character. . . . Thus even partners who are in love reach their most intense arousal as each focuses in on a particular trait of the partner—perhaps a particular element in the whole situation or on a particular body part.[8]

In discussing what causes people to choose between homosexuality and heterosexuality, he assigns primacy to physical issues:

It is a choice that stems from what will later be shown to be each individual's elaborately evolved sexual value system, a set of values that soon begins to eliminate the weaker alternatives while guiding a person none too gently toward the kinds of partners, the kinds of situations and sometimes even the kinds of acts that have become the salient imperatives of his highest sexual response.[9]

It is not irrelevant that true fetishism, a perversion in which sexual gratification can be achieved only by substituting an object or a body part (often the foot or hair) for a partner, occurs exclusively in men.

In this chapter I have presented very briefly some orienting descriptions of the masculine and feminine principles. At best it has been something on the order of an aerial photograph which can reveal shape, color, light and shadow, but not much more. One has seen the forest, but not the trees. Each person is unique, and the biological givenness of their sex with its psychological concomitants is normally modified by many other factors. These include not only such things as introversion and extroversion, intelligence, and personality type, but also the incredible range of experiences and circumstances to which they are exposed, including culture and education. Nevertheless, the fundamental difference between men and women is basic, and we are just beginning to learn the true nature of it—to discover that there is no sphere of human activity in which it is entirely irrelevant even though its effects are not those we once thought, and that the attitude we take to the difference may be at least as important as the difference itself.

7
Psychodynamics
of Female Homosexuality

The acquisition of basic gender identity for both boys and girls depends primarily on the fundamental process of separation from the mother. At first infants do not experience themselves as separate from their mothers any more than you and I experience ourselves as separate from, say, our liver or our lungs. Gradually, over the first few months of life, babies begin to experience themselves as less coextensive with their mothers, perhaps the way you and I feel about our arms and legs. As time goes on the sense of separate identity grows, but it takes up to two years for children to become really convinced that they are not part of their mothers—at least, to continue the metaphor, a lock of hair or a fingernail. Once the idea of physical separateness has been firmly established, however, the larger process is far from complete. The psychological and emotional separation takes years, and goes through recognizable stages. Although children vary greatly in their natural pace of acquiring independence, there are limits to how much each stage can safely be either forced or delayed. As we all know, from the example of married adults who feel the need to talk to their mothers daily on the telephone and who would not dream of living in a different town, some people never finish the process. For reasons which will soon become clearer, this pattern is commoner in women than in men.

Human development is not like climbing a mountain, where earlier stages of life might be compared to lower parts of the slope, places where one used to be but no longer is. It is much more like the growth of an onion, where the final shape of each layer is influenced by that of the one before and nothing is lost. This is why all of the experiences of infancy, childhood and adolescence are so important, and why, in cases where something has gone amiss, factors from more than one stage of development are usually found to have been operative. The task of separation from the mother, because the original closeness is rooted not in mere proximity but in actual identity, is absolutely basic for children of both sexes. No matter how tangled the relationship with the father may be, he is, from the start, *other.* The way in which the child relates to the mother at one stage will have effects on how the next stage is negotiated. This can work either for good or for ill. For instance, the mother who has, throughout her offspring's childhood, been able to be warm and loving without being clinging, supportive and helpful without being overprotective, and firm without being harshly critical, will be in a much better position to weather the storms of her child's adolescence than the mother who has consistently lost her balance in one or more of those ways. Mothers who are confident, proud of their own femininity, happy to be women, and neither jealous of or in rebellion against their husbands' masculinity will be able to do a much better job in helping both their boys and their girls to be comfortable and secure in their own sexual identity than will mothers who lack these qualities. The latter will unconsciously complicate the essential separation process.

The problem of the acquisition of basic gender identity can be seen, in these terms, to be very different for girls than for boys. A girl need only continue the original identification with her mother. To be sure, if her psychological development does not proceed beyond this stage, her function will be limited or impaired in various ways but her gender identity will not be threatened. Boys must go through a much more complicated struggle. This is analogous to what we saw earlier at the biological level. The basic human biological condition is female and special processes must take place in the embryo for maleness to develop. The same thing is true psychologically. This is why, as the Irving Beiber study demonstrated, the role of the father is so crucial in the development of normal male sexual identity. He is the *other* with whom the boy must learn to identify in order to extricate himself successfully from being the *same* as his mother.

Sometimes a mother, usually borderline psychotic, is so disturbed that she literally does not let her baby out of her arms for months at a time, and so perpetuates the total dependence on her which was characteristic of intrauterine life. Children of either sex who are treated this way are severely impaired in their development, of course. But when this is done to boys, the pathologically prolonged identification with the mother can permanently prevent them from being able to experience their biological maleness appropriately, and transsexualism may ensue in later life. Most often, in such cases, there has been no father in the household. Girls treated this way, whatever pathological patterns of helplessness and dependence may result, up to and including untreatable psychosis, still experience themselves as biologically female. This is why true transsexualism is unknown in women. (It should be noted that not all persons requesting sex change operations are transsexual in this sense. Once such operations become possible and publicized, people with a variety of psychosexual problems may be motivated to attempt to deal with their pathology in this way.)

Leaving aside these extreme cases, which have been sensationally publicized out of all proportion to their very rare incidence, let us consider what happens to the overwhelming majority of boys who are not in any doubt about their normal masculinity:

> The male child . . . *must* separate himself from the original, indispensable, nurturing mother and venture forth into a way of experiencing himself which is not her way, and which he cannot learn from her, either by example or by instruction. . . . He must learn to be different from her without this difference deteriorating into either antagonism or fear.[1]

The task of separation from the mother is an ongoing process which must be worked through afresh with each new stage of development. This is the underlying psychological need which is expressed in so many cultures through adolescent initiation rites for boys. In primitive societies these are often accompanied by periods of seclusion from female society, with the men taking the boys off to a separate place to impart the "secrets" of masculinity. In our culture these survive only in very diluted forms, such as Boy Scouts, Little League, and other bastions of youthful male privacy. Ill-advised women's liberationists who insist on admission of girls to such groups little realize that they are making the process of male maturation that much more difficult, and that they can expect perhaps even more trouble with the next generation of men than they have with this one.

Mothers who inquire too closely into the details of their adolescent sons' lives are compounding these difficulties. If they are not exacerbating a predisposition to homosexuality, they are at least reducing the eventual capacity for mature self-reliance and inviting that peculiarly exasperating kind of subtle male weakness which turns inappropriately to women, if not actually to mother, for rescue from many of life's unpleasant crises. Or, alternatively, women may be unfairly blamed when things go wrong. I think of the case of an extremely competent and successful man nearly thirty years old who, when the young woman he had been living with became pregnant and decided not to have an abortion, waxed extremely indignant at being thus inconvenienced—this in spite of his liberal pretensions to belief in women's rights; he then succeeded in *getting his mother* to try to persuade the young woman to change her mind! In Jungian terminology, such men are hampered in undertaking the necessary mature recognition and integration of their own unconscious contrasexual component, the *anima,* because they have been encouraged by ill-advised maternal intervention to continue not only to allow, but to expect, their mothers or other women to carry it for them. Such behavior is often perceived by contemporary feminists as male chauvinism when in fact it is mere weakness to which women themselves have been heavy contributors. Badgering such men to change their ways is worse than useless. They are best left alone until such time as life's lessons have taught them to grow up. A very experienced and wise European lady I know was once explaining to me the difference between a man and what she called a "man-boy." "A real man," she said, "always accepts consequences." How true!

This digression into another facet of male psychology is not irrelevant to the question of female homosexuality, since much of the lesbian feminist ideology is really directed to encouraging women to get out from under, literally as well as figuratively, this kind of male inadequacy masquerading as chauvinist superiority. Scratch a bully and you find a coward. Unfortunately for the present crop of marriageable young women, most men under the age of thirty-five in our culture are particularly prone to suffer from this kind of problem. This is because of the very wrong-headed views about the role of women and the nature of motherhood which gained wide acceptance after World War II. At that time, under the pressure of popularized distortions of Freudian theory and the concerted effort of Madison Avenue to create a class of people whose principal task in life was to be consumers, women were led to believe that the *only* appropriate objects of their energy and intelligence were their house and children.

Nor was this idea presented to them for implementation at the mental and spiritual level, but at the material one. We now have a whole generation of people who do not have enough sense to be shocked at such things as the successful Pillsbury slogan "Nothin' says lovin' like somethin' from the oven," let alone all those television commercials showing a woman apparently having an orgasm at the sight of a newly-waxed kitchen floor. Readers who doubt the deliberateness of this systematic emphasis on the material aspects of life should read Chapter Nine of Betty Friedan's well-known book, *The Feminine Mystique*,[2] and Professor William Bryan Key's book, *Subliminal Seduction*,[3] which expose the methods of the advertising industry. It is significant that the most common technique used to accomplish this economically greedy goal was the stimulation of people's anxiety about the profoundly basic issue of sexual identity and competence.

The generation of mothers thus brainwashed into doubt and insecurity about their own femininity and into over-involving themselves in the lives of their children, frequently sacrificed their own personal needs and development in order to do so. And as if all that were not enough, during this same period the trend to suburban living, which necessitated long commuting to work, removed fathers from the home to a degree hitherto unknown in any culture. In addition, many of these fathers had just returned from a long and terrible war. Because that war was perceived as a noble struggle to rescue civilization from unspeakable tyranny, the emotional aftereffects on the men who fought in it were insufficiently studied and recognized. Now, in the wake of the Vietnam war, which is perceived in an entirely different way, we are beginning to realize that the casualties represented by counting the dead and wounded are only the tip of the iceberg—war itself, quite apart from the justifiability of any particular conflict, is incalculably damaging to the personality and sensibilities of those who must participate in it, affecting especially the capacity to form and sustain intimate relationships. Such were the problems of the families which produced this generation containing a disproportionate number of comparatively weak men. It is easy to see that the essential conditions for healthy maturation of boys were seriously weakened; over-involved mothers and relatively distant fathers made the crucial maternal separation process and the acquisition of strong paternal ties very difficult.

The patriarchal system, already on the decline for excellent reasons, begins to look positively ridiculous rather than merely obsolete when it is being implemented by insecure men who have trouble taking responsibility. It is one thing to defer to men who have earned the right to be respected—even if one's own rights have been neglected; it is quite another to be urged to engage in mindless phallic worship.

Young women, whose own growth was also hampered by these postwar conditions in ways which we will discuss presently, frequently have become disillusioned when attempting to select mates from the damaged pool of candidates. Some, after a series of unfortunate affairs or a disastrous marriage, have turned to older men. This is not always because, as some of their traditional therapists try to tell them, they have unresolved attachments to their fathers, but because only in that age group can they find a truly reliable man, one mature enough to be looking for a real mate, not just a mother in reserve. Quite understandably, others either settle for a man they cannot really respect or else reject men altogether. Some of these, supported by the more positive values of the women's liberation movement, turn to a life of what Margaret Adams calls "single blessedness."[4] A few turn to lesbianism.

While it is probably true that no woman will select this option unless her childhood and adolescent experiences have made her vulnerable, the easier availability of mature men would provide her with an opportunity to heal these early wounds rather than rip them open. In the last few years I have seen several young women of this type, the *primary* cause of whose homosexual behavior appears to be sociological rather than psychological. Naturally, this kind of anecdotal clinical impression does not have the the force and authority of systematic controlled studies of large numbers of subjects such as the ones on male homosexuality previously cited; but it does raise questions to which future research might profitably be addressed. Some preliminary support for my view, however, is to be found in the *"Redbook* Report" on female sexuality previously referred to, which notes that ten percent of the separated, divorced and widowed group has had at least one sexual experience with other women.

Unfortunately, in spite of the size of the sample (one hundred thousand respondents compared to eight thousand women studied by Kinsey), the *"Redbook* Report" does not give us definitive answers on the general incidence of female homosexuality. *Redbook* readers do not constitute a random sample of the general population; the questionnaire itself was slanted toward married women. However, there were answers from a wide variety of economic and educational levels so the figures are at least indicative. Three percent of high school graduates, four percent of those with some college, and five percent of those with college or graduate degrees reported at least one homosexual encounter since the age of eighteen, but for two-thirds of these women it had happened only once. It is therefore likely that at most three percent of women in this country are true homosexuals according to the definition given in Chapter Two. This coheres with

Kinsey's finding that female homosexuality is only about half as common as the male variety. The reason for this surely lies in the fact that, as we saw earlier in this chapter, the problem of acquiring and maintaining sexual identity is more difficult for males than for females.

In female as well as male homosexuality unresolved problems related to the three basic issues of infantile dependency needs, difficulties with dominance and submission, and fear of the opposite sex are all operative. Due to the biological and psychological differences between men and women which have already been discussed, both the psychodynamic and the behavioral patterns which result may be quite different. In addition, the familiar problems of stereotyped role expectations influencing child-rearing practices, and the various ways in which the feminine principle is devalued in our culture further alter the manifestations of homosexuality in women.

The primary sense of identity with the mother provides all but a tiny fraction of women with a secure sense of their natural femaleness. In the rare cases where this does not happen, it is the result of extremely abnormal parenting. More common are those cases where the child knows perfectly well that she is a girl, but resents it. She may deal with this by trying to deny it, by hoping that somehow she may grow a penis, or by imagining that she used to have one but lost it. She also vigorously shuns those activities which her particular environment defines as specifically feminine and pursues those which are defined as masculine. The more narrowly femininity is defined, particularly by the mother, the more likely such a pattern is to emerge. A small girl who is physically vigorous and energetic, fearless and curious, will be especially resentful and frustrated if she is raised in a home where girls are expected to be quiet, dainty and clean all the time, uninterested in sports other than games like hopscotch, and principally interested in those indoor games which mimic homemaking and motherhood. But even such treatment in early childhood need not lead to a permanent masculinity complex if there are compensating factors. More enlightened views on the part of teachers and of mothers in homes where she goes to play are helpful.

More important, however, is the way in which the girl's mother values her own femininity, since this will inevitably influence the way in which her daughter will value hers. Some mothers are stereotypically "feminine," but reveal their underlying negative attitudes by such things as favoring their sons over their daughters, or treating their daughters as rivals for male attention. As with men, the influence of the father may well be determinative. Fathers who are confident and secure in their own masculine identity and who are able to show both concern and affection to their female children and to encourage them to find their own independent interests can counteract the influence of mothers who are undermining their daughters' individuality and self-esteem.

The various psychodynamic patterns which can be grouped under the general heading of a masculinity complex, one sufficiently severe to produce the type of lesbian who consciously lives out a caricature of "masculine" behavior both in and out of bed, are relatively rare. Such women can be overtly sadistic; with or without that manifestation they are unduly aggressive, tough and competitive. This can arise either from great admiration of men coupled with contempt for women, or from fear. Usually both attitudes coexist. Here the dynamic seems to be "I am afraid of men, it's not safe to be a woman, therefore I will pretend I am a man." Sometimes these women have a history of rape at an early age or have grown up in a household where a masochistic or inadequate mother was consistently and grossly mistreated by her husband or other men. Another variety of this general pattern is one in which a very "masculine" woman may adjust well in the world of men, particularly in work situations, where she may be accepted (with varying degrees of amused condescension) as "one of the boys." She is likely to treat more feminine co-workers, if any, with contempt or antagonism.

These cases center, to some extent, around issues of dominance and submission and are not so common in women as they are in men. This is because women are not usually socialized in a way which includes any expectation that aggressiveness, competitiveness and a high degree of self-assertion ought to form a significant part of their sexual identity. In such cases there is also a profound conviction of basic female inferiority, which is usually unconscious, but which always emerges sooner or later in long-term psychotherapy. This is true even when the symptom for which treatment is begun is unrelated to questions of sexuality.

We saw earlier that in prisons for men the pattern of homosexuality which frequently emerges is one which tends to establish the "pecking order" among the inmates. In women's prisons, the situation is quite different. Here the network of relationships is most often modeled on the family, the women according to their temperament and particular type of lesbianism taking the roles of father or protector, mother, children, and sometimes grandparents, aunts and other relations. The detail with which normal family structure is caricatured is remarkable, sometimes including the incest taboo as well as other cultural features. At the other, less pathological end of the scale there is good reason to suppose that stable, long-term relationships between lesbians occur more frequently than they do between male homosexuals, among whom such associations are quite rare.

The psychological basis for most lesbianism lies more in the other two areas: unresolved issues around dependency upon the mother and fear of heterosexuality. Some readers will be old enough to remember the proverb, "A son is a son 'til he gets him a wife, a daughter's a daughter all of her life." There is a great deal of truth in this saying. Taken as a concise description of normal maturation, it underlines a man's need, previously discussed, to separate from his mother and to be able to form an adult attachment to a mate. This has always been known and understood and is exemplified by St. Paul's quotation from Genesis, "For this cause shall a man leave his father and mother, and shall be joined unto his wife . . ." (Ephesians 5:31). Male maturity and independence have always been valued.

The second half of the proverb points both to the strength and to the weakness of the daughter's different position. The strength is what I think the women's movement is reaching for, but often misses, in the concept of "sisterhood." There is a sense of confidence, of relaxed power, which is the peculiar birthright of women. This power needs no special assertion, requires no strident voice to declare itself. It does not depend for reinforcement on successfully vanquished opponents, or on obstacles courageously overcome. It knows too much about blood and death to romanticize either, or even to fear them very much. It is the power of *source,* and at least one great male author also perceived it as the power of *goal:* "Das ewige Weibliche zieht uns an" ("The eternal feminine draws us forward"), the closing lines of Goethe's *Faust.* It is no accident that in the dreams of individuals as well as in myths (which are the dreams of the race) feminine figures are always chosen to represent the soul. Today's feminist writers are often outraged, and male theologians often embarrassed, by some of the medieval debates on the question of whether or not women had souls. What is forgotten is that one of the most important arguments was that the reason women cannot be said to *have* a soul is because they *are* soul. This is a way, inadequate of course to the exigencies of our time and generation, of referring to the special power of the feminine which I have tried to describe. Women I have known, both in and out of therapy, on the occasion of getting in touch with this power typically have an unforgettable, numinous dream. In it there appears a veritable procession of all the women in their life—friends, mother, grandmother, costumed figures whom they know to be their unknown, distant ancestresses, and even women from the Bible or female deities from various mythologies. Their daughters and grand-daughters, born or unborn, may also appear. Sisterhood is a pale word, inadequate to convey the meaning behind such dreams. I can-not begin to put into words the timeless feeling of peace and stability which the realization of this participation in the archetype of Woman brings.

It is clear that physical motherhood and the ability to attract men sexually just by one's very being are *part* of this power. But women who have settled for the destructive falsehood which claims that that is all there is to it have sold their priceless feminine birthright for a mess of materialist and sexual pottage. Their ability to appreciate themselves as real women, fully human, an indispensable half of the image of God, is seriously weakened. We have seen that postwar conditions in the United States contributed heavily to the contemporary exacerbation of this chronic problem. When deprived of their own sense of themselves and of much necessary intellectual, emotional, and spiritual nourishment, mothers are tempted to devour their children instead. The effects on boys have already been described.

What happens to the daughters of such women? They fail to receive from their mothers that wonderful, proud sense of timeless continuity which carries real strength, and so the second half of the proverb, ". . . a daughter's a daughter all of her life," instead of referring to that beautiful fearlessness, may become a suffocating trap in which everything is feared, even beauty itself. In the introduction to her very fine book, *Daughters and Mothers, Mothers and Daughters,* Signe Hammer describes the contemporary problem well.

> Home and work are now considered to be mutually exclusive, and our society has not been in a hurry to reconcile them. Being feminine has come to mean attracting a husband and raising his children. . . . The scope of activity allowed for in the feminine role has narrowed to the point of near nonexistence, except for child care.
>
> As the scope of women's work diminished, the idea of childhood, and of the importance of good mothering developed. And here we have another paradox: women who themselves are not allowed to assume adult roles as persons in our society . . . are expected to socialize the new generation. As we shall see, this has presented a particular problem for daughters. A vicious cycle has developed in which women who were not encouraged to grow up raise daughters who are not encouraged to grow up either . . .[5]

The family behavior patterns which have been found in the background of lesbians are exaggerations of these difficulties. Some women have serious, unsatisfied dependency needs because they received inadequate mothering during infancy and childhood. The homosexual adaptation in such cases is essentially a regressive attempt to secure the safety and pleasure of identification with the maternal principle. When there are several daughters in a family, only one of whom was rejected or inadequately mothered and later became a lesbian, investigation usually reveals that at this particular birth a son was urgently desired, or that for other reasons the child did not conform to the pattern of temperament and behavior which her mother thought suitable or desirable in girls. Because of this, she grew up with a lonely sense of exclusion from the intimate feminine world shared by her mother and sisters and her eventual lesbianism is an attempt to make up for this loss.

Other lesbians have been abnormally mothered in a very different way; they have been "erotically seduced by prolonged infancy."[6] The sensuous pleasures of total involvement with the mother have been indulged to the exclusion of the development of any capacity to be independent and separate from this kind of support. In adult life, these women are likely to select women older than themselves as partners in order to reproduce as nearly as possible the ecstatic conditions of infancy.

Women who have never adequately relinquished their infantile attachment to their mothers find it more difficult to take the subsequent steps in psychosexual development which are required for the establishment of a satisfactory heterosexual adjustment. This is particularly true since some degree of abnormal fathering can also always be demonstrated. Some fathers are so fixated on the relationship with their wives that the children are ignored. Others are so preoccupied with their work that the entire family is ignored. In either case, the growing girl is deprived of any meaningful relationship with her father, and this makes any subsequent connection with men difficult. Where the father has been exclusively attending to his wife, the daughter perceives herself as her mother's defeated rival for male attention and this undermines her self-confidence to a crippling degree. The chances are good that in such instances the mother's own insecurity about herself causes her to perceive the situation in exactly the same way—only through successful competition with other women, even her own daughter, can she retain her precarious hold on her self-esteem. Such a mother may be flirtatious and seductive with her daughter's boyfriends if the girl attempts to have any.

Fathers who are sadistic or harshly critical with their daughters can also contribute to an eventual homosexual adaptation. This can be the beginning of a lifelong fear of men, especially if the mother fails to come to her daughter's rescue. In other, still more pathological cases, a father's seductiveness with his daughter can also contribute to a wholesale rejection of men, especially if this is unaccompanied by any evidence of valuing her for other than sexual reasons. Mothers who undervalue their own femininity may contribute to the girl's sense of helplessness in the face of such treatment by instilling a generalized fear of men, as well as by expressing disgust for sex and exaggerating the dangers and unpleasantness of childbirth. It is easy to understand why such girls might decide that it just isn't worth it to grow up. Only the world of women, of mothers and daughters, is seen as safe, comfortable, and trustworthy.

Sometimes a woman does not turn to lesbianism until well into her adult years or even middle age, often after marrying and having children. Even though this has the appearance of a free choice, it is actually an escape from a life of disappointment and frustration which has finally become intolerable. Of the several possible solutions to such a dilemma, the regression to the earlier world of peaceful mother-daughter relationship is the only one she had the strength to undertake. In spite of strident rhetoric to the contrary, most lesbians believe in the overall superiority of men. They may consider women to excel in sensitivity and gentleness, but they also see these desirable and pleasant qualities as fatally contaminated by weakness. In any intimate association with men this sense of female inferiority is underlined, whereas intimacy with other women enables them to at least bypass it and sometimes actually to deny it. Of course there can be no question that these ideas, even if only held unconsciously, are powerfully influenced by the position of women in society. Nevertheless it is equally clear that, for a sense of female inferiority to eventuate in a committed homosexual adaptation, more specific, individual malign influences must have been brought to bear on a woman's development.

Homosexual behavior in adolescence is just as significant to women as it is to men, but there is an additional twist. The emotional and social maturity of adolescent girls tends to outstrip that of boys. There are many reasons why sexual experience at too young an age is harmful, not the least of which is that it places a great strain on the development of these children who have not yet completed the tasks of acquiring a strong ego and the accompanying capacity for mature independence. Girls caught in these situations frequently discover that they have to mother their immature male sex partners. Not unreasonably, some of them decide that, if mothering and sex must go together, it would at least be preferable to mother each other, where it is more likely to be appreciated and valued. Boys of that age simultaneously demand and reject mothering––they are notorious for biting the hand that feeds, however unintentionally.

Regardless of the frustration and despair which may be caused by disappointing and traumatic circumstances, no woman who is properly related to her own contrasexual component, her *animus*, ever becomes committed to a homosexual adaptation. When her development is not thwarted in some way, the *animus* is friend, guide, lightbearer, but never master. But if there are problems, the woman may identify with this archetype or, in other words, she is possessed by her *animus*. When this process begins at a very young age, which it is all too likely to do when the parenting has been as abnormal as that described above, it may become impossible for the girl to develop a strong, healthy feminine ego. In adult life this may, in extreme cases, lead to the patterns of immaturity characterized by selfishness and jealousy, which in Freudian terms are referred to as narcissism. If the family patterns have predisposed such a girl to the homosexual adaptation, she will be the kind of lesbian who is unable to maintain stable relationships, who creates jealous, recriminating scenes with her lovers. But even when ego development has not been so severely damaged as that, it is still "the animus who promotes incestuous desires from daughter to mother, and from mother to daughter."[8] Although the archetype of the *animus* is universal in women, the particular way in which it is constellated in the psyche of individual women is heavily dependent upon her experiences with the actual men in her life, particularly during childhood. This is why the influence of the father is so important. But I have known a case where incestuous relations forced on a girl by a bullying brother seem to have been the determinative influence. Of course such a thing is most unlikely to occur if the parents are competent observers and guides to their children.

It is utterly impossible for something like the feminist movement to evolve without the active participation of the *animus* in each woman involved in it. The type of woman who is conscious only of her stereotypically feminine side and is content to project her *animus* onto the men in her environment, getting them to carry it all for her, is just not the type of woman who ever gets involved in such things. Her consciousness has not yet been raised. But there is an enormous difference between the feminist activities of women who are to one degree or another possessed by their *animus,* and those of women who are the secure mistresses of their own psychological house. For these women, the *animus* is more like a consultant who is called on for advice and illumination, but to whom the responsibility for the final decision is never shifted. All feminists are involved in the recovery of the feminine principle and in the renewed enjoyment of feminine power and solidarity. But only those who are *animus*-possessed link this task with antagonism toward men or with contempt for women who genuinely prefer a traditional lifestyle, not to mention the disturbed radical few who link feminine liberation with homosexuality. This is a tragic mistake, one which, for those unfortunate enough to be seduced by it, makes impossible the true enjoyment of real feminine strength.

8
Treatment of Homosexuality

Before proceeding with the discussion of treatment, we must consider those published reports which claim to refute the idea that homosexuals are necessarily more neurotic or less adapted than heterosexuals. Most of this work relies on one or both of two basic premises. The first premise is that psychotherapists only see those people who do have some personality disturbance which is severe enough for them to seek help. That homosexuality itself could cause trouble, were it not disapproved of by society, is denied. Such symptoms as are found and treated are either independent of the sexual orientation or else are a direct result of the punitive treatment and ostracism which the patient has suffered because of it. The argument further runs that homosexuals who, in spite of these serious social handicaps, have managed to resist their pernicious influence, or who have no independently occurring neurosis of a different nature, are simply not seen by psychiatrists. The conclusion is drawn that it is inaccurate and misleading to assume that what is learned about the psychodynamics of those neurotic persons who do present themselves for treatment could possibly have any bearing on the psychological processes of people who, though homosexual, have no other recognizable disorder.

The second premise upon which these arguments for the normality of homosexuality rest is that all that has been learned in the last hundred years about the psychosexual development of human beings is simply irrelevant to the question of homosexuality. That is explained either as a congenital disposition, as inevitable and as value-free as, say, eye color, or else as an acquired taste with no more pathological or moral significance than food or color preferences.

From the viewpoint of strict logic, these arguments are circular. They presuppose the very thing they purport to be proving: namely, that homosexuality in and of itself is not pathological. Once that assumption is made the presence of this condition apart from other symptoms is taken as proof of its lack of pathology! Perhaps the fallacious structure of the argument can be clarified through an analogy. Let us suppose that a group of people prefers to think that gray hair is *not* a sign of aging. These people might try to argue that, because gray hair is sometimes seen in young people, it therefore has nothing whatsoever to do with the aging process. This is obviously not sufficient proof; all it demonstrates is that in some people gray hair is the *only* sign of aging. To establish the new hypothesis would require new biochemical evidence about the nature of hair. Unless that were forthcoming, it would be perfectly accurate to refer to afflicted young people as prematurely gray, even if there were no evidence of an accelerated aging process in any other part of their body. You just cannot prove that something is normal by saying that, if it ever occurs apart from other pathology, it cannot be abnormal in itself. Such logic would require a person to have two diseases in order to be sick! What is at issue is not the scientific evidence which, as we have seen in previous chapters, supports the view that homosexuality results from distortions of the normal psychological growth process. What is really involved is a *prior value judgment* about homosexuality.

It has, however, been alleged that, because various experiments have failed to distinguish homosexuals from heterosexuals, no imputation of pathology can be successfully defended. One study in particular is cited over and over again in the professional literature and in books by homosexual apologists. It is worth reviewing in some detail.

In 1958 psychologist Evelyn Hooker studied thirty homosexual men not in psychiatric treatment and compared them with thirty heterosexual men. Psychological tests were given, in particular the

Rorschach, which is the well-known "ink-blot test." An independent team of consultants who had never seen the subjects read the test results. They were unable to distinguish the homosexuals from the heterosexuals; the conclusion was drawn that there may therefore be nothing especially neurotic about homosexuality.[1]

There are several criticisms of this study which make the inferences drawn from it completely unjustifiable. In the first place, the sample is much too small. In fairness to Dr. Hooker it should be stated that she intended this as a pilot study only. But, eighteen years later, attempts to replicate the work on a larger scale have not yet succeeded.

More important than these statistical objections is the fact that the study involves a misunderstanding of the proper use and limitations of the Rorschach test. It is questionable to have test protocols or verbal transcriptions of the subject's responses to the cards read by someone other than the person who administered the test. Sophisticated and refined testing procedure calls for careful evaluation of body language, facial expression, tone of voice, and other clues to the subject's responses. These nuances are of course absent from simple transcripts. Beyond this, the Rorschach test was never intended, and in fact does not work, as an exclusive and "last word" diagnostic tool. It is simply not the psychological analog of an X-ray, for instance. From the beginning of its use, it has been known that the Rorschach does not specifically expose the homosexual adaptation; in fact, it cannot reliably distinguish men from women. What it can and does do is point to the underlying issues—fear, dependency, and problems with authority. What it does not show specifically is how a given person has built up defenses to cope with these, and certainly not what external life pattern may have evolved.

I do not deny that there may be, and probably are, persons with the homosexual adaptation who do not suffer from any other obvious dysfunction and are perhaps not likely to. But the presence of such people does not speak to the question of how they developed their homosexuality in the first place, nor does it address the issue of the normality of that behavior. What it does speak to is their own ability to muster the rest of their strengths in such a way as to prevent this dysfunction from impoverishing the quality of the rest of their life. There is, after all, no one who has had a perfect childhood and adolescence; therefore everyone's adult psychological organization includes compensations for and defenses against disturbing influences, as well as more or less successful resolutions of early conflict. An example may clarify this point. Consider two people, each having suffered an attack of paralytic poliomyelitis in childhood. One may be able to muster the body's recuperative and compensatory powers in such a way as to overcome nearly all the effects in adult life, whereas the other may be an invalid. There could also be many intermediate adaptations. The existence of the otherwise healthy polio victim says nothing to contradict the idea that polio is abnormal. It does tell something about the general vigor of the person's constitution as well as their determination to deal constructively with their handicap.

Considering the history of the therapeutic approach to homosexuals, it is perhaps not surprising that they should eventually have staged a wholesale revolt against the psychiatric profession. In an interesting review article, Dr. Samuel Hadden, who has devoted his professional career to sexual disorders, writes the following:

> During the years of Freud's pessimistic influence, many afflicted homosexuals came to psychiatrists, but few of the psychiatrists made much of an attempt to help the homosexual alter a pattern of behavior that society found unacceptable. Influenced by the authoritarian words of the Viennese master, most psychiatrists who were approached by homosexuals for treatment told their patients, in effect, "The only thing I can do is to help you live with it more comfortably"—a laudable goal, perhaps, but one that often did little more for the patient than intensify the despair he was already experiencing.

> Many psychiatrists, in fact, resorted only to exhortation and moralizing. They shared the attitude of the community towards the homosexual: he was a revolting, disgusting pervert. Ministers often held similar attitudes, but they usually were not so aggressive in their denunciations as many of the psychiatrists.[2]

In the same paper, Dr. Hadden points out that in the twenty years between 1930 and 1950 only twelve articles dealing with homosexuality appeared in the *American Journal of Psychiatry,* and not one of those dealt with psychotherapy of the condition. Until Irving Bieber and his associates published *Homosexuality* in 1962, it was not widely recognized that psychoanalytic techniques could usefully be applied not only to the understanding, but also to the treatment of homosexuality. Since that time, many reports have appeared in the professional literature and a number of books on the subject have been published. These have dealt not only with the psychodynamics, but also, and at great and encouraging length, with treatment.

What has been learned from this work? Approximately thirty percent of male homosexuals who come to psychotherapy for *any reason* (not just for help with their sexual preference) can be converted to the heterosexual adaptation. As explained in Chapter Seven, not as much is systematically known about female homosexuality as about the condition in men. What is known gives no reason to doubt that the treatment of women is any less successful, but the relative unavailability of statistically reliable evidence does not permit the statement to be made with the same categorical confidence as in the case of men.

Current homosexual rhetoric might well leave the average person with the impression that when homosexuals seek help from conventional sources with any symptom whatever, therapists give first priority to the homosexual issue and badger the patients into trying to change their sexual orientation. If such an approach were ever actually taken it would be, at the least, useless, and often actually harmful. Nothing could be farther from the truth of what really happens.

One of the first principles of psychotherapy is that one must not make premature interpretations. By this is meant that the therapist must meet patients and establish sympathetic rapport with them on their own ground before any attempt is made to change anything. Progress must be made one step at a time, and no interpretation or suggestion should be made which does not naturally proceed from what patients themselves have already said, understood, and accepted. It often happens, not only with homosexuality but with other disorders as well, that after the first two or three interviews the therapist has an excellent idea of just what is wrong, and could give an accurate, lengthy, and detailed description of the psychodynamics, diagnosis, prognosis, and probable course of therapy. It would, however, be worse than useless to tell all that to the patient then and there.

A wise teacher of mine once said, "We do not treat the patients with what we know, but with what we are." This is not to say that the years of study and experience do not provide therapists with a conceptual frame of reference which they must have in order to make sense of the confusion and irrationality which the patient presents. But no patient ever gets well because the doctor has figured out what is wrong. Patients must learn to *feel differently* about themselves and this can only come about through a corrective emotional experience which is based on the interpersonal transaction between the patient and the therapist. If the therapist does not really care, if the therapist is not really involved, patients continue to feel isolated and unworthy no matter how much they may have learned intellectually about the causes of such feelings.[3]

It should be borne in mind that *no* symptom or neurotic pattern which the patient does not experience as unacceptable or troublesome has much likelihood of being the object of successful therapeutic intervention. This is one reason why the incidence of improvement or recovery for patients who are referred by courts or dragged in unwillingly by their relatives is so disappointingly low. The central importance of the patient's motivation and initiative is not confined to homosexuality.

Needless to say, a therapist who has feelings of revulsion toward homosexuals is not likely to be of much help; but it is incorrect to say that any therapist who believes that homosexuality is dysfunctional is "biased" and therefore doing more harm than good, as Tripp and others have claimed. That there are therapists whose own personal attitudes make it difficult for them to take a truly therapeutic stance with homosexuals cannot be denied. But this problem is not confined to homosexuality. For instance, I myself am not able to treat parents who batter their children. I know intellectually that these people need help, and even what their general problems are likely to be. But the anger and outrage I feel toward anyone who abuses children is so great that I am completely unable to form a therapeutic alliance with them. Therapists who have a parallel problem with homosexuality should refer homosexuals coming to them for treatment—no matter what symptom is being presented—to someone who can see the whole patient without being blinded by a particular facet.

Dr. Lawrence Hatterer, in his book on the therapy of male homosexuality, gives the clearest presentation I have seen of which cases have a good prognosis and which do not. As I have explained above, it is never good therapeutic technique to try to deal directly with the homosexual symptom unless or until the patient expresses a wish or need to do so. But regardless of whether heterosexual adaptation can be achieved, the homosexual patient with other difficulties can usually be helped toward a better level of adjustment. As Dr. Hatterer says:

> The most therapeutic attitude for a therapist is that he can help the patient achieve any one of a number of possible goals within the context of the depth, duration, and nature of his past and present homosexuality. The patient's homosexual history and habits inevitably dictate what attitudes are most realistic in any therapeutic collaboration. In treatment of a patient who is past thirty-five and whose homosexual past is extensive, goals have to be modest and limited. With a young person whose homosexual history is limited to brief transient contacts and essentially is ego-alien, a therapist can assume that re-adaptation to heterosexuality is highly possible.[4]

There are a number of different psychological vocabularies in which successful therapy may be conducted. The Freudian terminology is the one with which most people are familiar, at least to some extent. It is likely to focus primarily on childhood experiences and to elucidate them in terms of the classic concepts of oral and anal gratifications and frustrations, resolution of the Oedipal conflict, and the psychological mechanisms of repression, sublimation, reaction formation, identification with the aggressor, and others. Jungian therapy is more likely to focus on complexes associated with the archetypes and, in the case of homosexuality, special attention will be devoted to the particular constellation and function of the *animus* or *anima*. Other "talking therapies" include existential analysis, logotherapy, and many more. Some therapists use an eclectic approach, borrowing from all of these systems to suit the needs of a particular case. Successful results have been reported with all of these methods.

There are, however, a number of people for whom this essential process of prolonged, sophisticated, and subtle introspection is prohibitively difficult or uncongenial. They are either too extroverted, or have such rigid defense mechanisms that the primarily verbal psychotherapies work very poorly. For patients of this kind, the behavior modification approach often works better, using various kinds of conditioning techniques. Occasionally, hypnotic therapy is also helpful with such people. Good results have been reported with all of these methods, as well as with the more conventional psychotherapies described above.

More important than the particular theoretical framework is the attitude of the therapist. The ability not to be horrified by the symptom is essential. The homosexual's inability to perceive himself as securely competent to assert himself appropriately, or to compete successfully with other men in the world, or to be unthreatened by loss of autonomous selfhood in intimate contacts with women are all characteristic of male homosexuals. Such difficulties, singly or in combination, both lead to and are aggravated by a deep-seated sense of inferiority which often takes on the proportions of suicidal despair. If the therapist is unable to be sympathetic and understanding about the homosexual symptom, these feelings are intensified.

Beyond that, it is extremely important for the therapist to resist the temptation to make decisions for the patient, or to give too much concrete advice about how to manage various aspects of his life. These patients are often extremely subtle in manipulating the therapist into such a position. This generally comes about during a phase of what is known as "positive transference" in which the therapist is more or less unconsciously cast in the role of "good parent" to counteract the influence of the "bad parent" whose attitudes and behavior were so damaging during childhood and youth. While this may be an improvement in many ways and, in some cases, may be a necessary stage of therapy, it is extremely important to move beyond it as rapidly as possible. The *really* good parent, after all, is the one who encourages children to grow into real independence, real self-sufficiency; the one whose voice of experience giving advice is just that—advice, not a covert imperative which children disregard at their peril. This calls for an enormous amount of support of the patient's initially halting and tentative moves toward growth, and encouragement to seek out those in the community who will give similar support. These general principles hold true whether the patient is one for whom the goal of treatment is re-adaptation to heterosexuality, or one whose therapeutic goal is to move away from the depressing and sometimes dangerous impersonality of a succession of quick homosexual pick-ups to an ability to form a stable, rewarding relationship with a more mature homosexual companion.

One of the most unfortunate effects of the current homosexual activism is that those who really wish to undertake the process of change or improvement are often treated with bitter hostility by their former associates. As Dr. Charles Socarides has said, homosexuals were formerly buried by being considered untreatable pariahs; now they are in danger of burial again by being called normal. In response to an article I wrote about homosexuality, I received the following letter from someone (not a psychotherapist) whose work took him to several institutions of higher learning and provided him with an opportunity for close contacts with students.

While in ——— I became very much aware of what I suspected. A number of students at ——— who are practicing homosexuals (so to speak), feel dreadful about it but also feel that they *ought* to rejoice in it. In short, it seems to me that such a place as ——— or ——— (or even society in general) is damaging . . . many by providing no support for them to seek release from this burden of unhappiness. On the contrary, it supports them in a pattern of life which, at some deep level, they know is bad and makes them unhappy.

I can wholeheartedly support this observation from experiences in my own practice.

In his book Tripp makes the astonishing and totally untrue claim that *no* cures of the homosexual symptom have ever been reported. In essence, he is accusing scores of conscientious and responsible psychiatrists and psychologists of falsifying their data. This is utterly outrageous and I find it difficult to excuse or explain, even on the grounds that Tripp's definition of what constitutes homosexuality is clearly very different, as we shall see, not only from that given in Chapter Two, but also from any of the usually understood meanings of the term.

For Tripp, anyone who has even an occasional homosexual dream or fantasy is to be thought of as a homosexual. Such a definition is ludicrously broad. After all, if one has a fantasy about killing one's mother-in-law that does not make one a murderer! He is taking homosexuality as the basic condition, reversing the charge on universal human experience, since he does not consider that some heterosexual acts or fantasy make a person heterosexual. He is also denying (and I find this denial incomprehensible coming from a psychotherapist) that sex, like food, money, and many other universals, is often used symbolically in fantasy and dreams; it may appear in unusual or even bizarre forms which it would be absurd to attempt to understand literally.

Those who are preferentially homosexual, or who advert to episodic homosexuality under certain kinds of stress, are not, after all, the only ones to have problems related to competition, feelings of inferiority, or occasional trouble getting along with women. Men who are thoroughly and happily heterosexual may choose a homosexual dream symbol as a succinct way of expressing such anxieties, and this is particularly likely to occur when they are making a determined, conscious effort to avoid or deny the important issues. To have a homosexual dream is sufficiently shocking, and even frightening in many instances, so that they are forced to come to grips with their practical problem. I have also had several women patients who used lesbian dream symbols to express their longing for a warm and supportive relationship with their mothers which, in their conscious life, they were concerned for one reason or another to deny.

But these considerations do not apply only to homosexual symbolism. Unfortunately, if one has a dream or fantasy that one has won the Nobel Prize, this does not mean that one is "really" a genius. There is no illicit act, from murder through incest, rape, and the entire catalogue of the perverse and the bizarre which may not appear in the dreams of perfectly respectable people. Fortunately, this does not mean that they are likely to commit such acts in waking life. I am sure that Tripp himself would not tell a patient who reported a dream about cannibalism, for instance, that he "really" was a cannibal!

One does not have to consult the casebooks of psychotherapists to recognize the essentially symbolic character of dreams and fantasies. I am sure that all readers in the habit of recalling their dreams can verify what I have said from their own experiences. To select one such symbol, homosexuality, and, processing it through the fallacy of misplaced concreteness, to insist that it be taken as a literal statement of a person's manifest sexual inclinations, is flagrantly irresponsible and intellectually dishonest.

It is to such lengths that Tripp is reduced in attempting to back up his claim that no cures have ever been reported. But he does not stop there. His chapter, "The Question of Psychotherapy," abounds with other contradictions and failures of logic. For example, in one paragraph he says that therapists unbiased against the condition, either because they are former sex researchers or because they are themselves homosexual "almost invariably note that if they had seen homosexuality first and only in clinical examples, they would probably have agreed with the standard opinions."[5] But a mere six pages later he claims that the only reason patients ever give the history which supports those "standard opinions," is that they have familiarized themselves with psychiatric theories and are attempting to tell the therapist who believes in them what he wants to hear! He actually refers to such cases as "drab, sad, largely stage-managed reports."[6] Why have these patients evidently given the same sort of history to "unbiased" therapists as well? And has he actually advanced his cause by thus taking for granted a self-defeating passivity sufficiently extreme to cause hundreds of homosexual men to fabricate or embellish their histories for the gratification of therapists who are being *paid* to listen and be helpful?

Those who have not read or heard of Tripp's book may wonder why I am spending so much time discussing it. Many of my professional colleagues, including some whose work has been egregiously misrepresented by Tripp, consider his slipshod methods and lack of scholarship beneath intellectual contempt and have refused to even dignify his work with a reply. But many other people less familiar with the field, and particularly those whose education has been in the humanities rather than in the sciences, have apparently been dazzled by the mere presence of 292 footnotes. It has been quoted as an "authoritative" source in subsequent books and periodicals, many of which erroneously identify Tripp as a faculty member of the State University of New York. This is one of those peculiar accidents of the publishing industry by which an entirely unfounded rumor gets repeated so often that it is taken for fact. In the 1975 directory of the American Psychological Association the accurate biographical information supplied by Tripp himself makes no such claim, either past or present.

Increasingly, the terminological problem makes discussion of cure, as well as incidence, extremely difficult. "The Gay Manifesto," for instance, defines homosexuality as "the capacity to love someone of the same sex." Many authors have accepted this idea, in whole or in part, and this makes understanding their work a tedious chore. Such definitions do violence to the precision and subtlety of the English language as well as to common sense, and make the much needed exchange of meaningful information and informed opinion about homosexuality excessively difficult. The capacity to love—to care deeply for others in enduring relationships—is a function not of one's sexual orientation nor of the gender of the person one loves, but is rather a function of one's maturity. There are loving as well as loveless people among both homosexuals and heterosexuals.

Further complicating the terminological problem is the inaccurate and misleading way in which Kinsey's *Sexual Behavior in the Human*

Male (1948) is quoted by contemporary authors. Kinsey devised what he called a heterosexual-homosexual seven-point rating scale: men were given a rating of zero if they had no physical contacts and no "psychic responses" (undefined further) with other men; at the other end of the scale, a rating of six was given to those who had physical and/or "psychic responses" only with other men. Behavior which had taken place in adolescence was included in each rating. For statistical purposes this was no doubt useful and led to information (at that time new and interesting) about the incidence of homosexual acts, all of which was presented in a series of elaborate statistical tables and graphs. His research was not addressed to the circumstances under which such behavior took place, nor to any psychodynamic patterns. Now we find books and articles by homosexual apologists or by other authors whose facility in interpreting the significance of statistical studies seems severely limited, in which Kinsey's work is taken to mean that all men are on a continuum and very few are either exclusively homosexual or heterosexual. This interpretation does violence to Kinsey's own statistics. Examination of the graph below, taken from Kinsey's original book, shows that, far from an even continuum of sexual orientation, there is a radical discontinuity between adult men who are heterosexual and those who are not.[7]To use the word *continuum* about a seven-point scale on which ninety percent of the subjects have two of the ratings and the other five ratings are distributed among only ten percent of the subjects is extremely misleading.

It must be remembered that Kinsey's work came long before any of the psychodynamic studies cited in Chapter Five. Even so, it is clear that Kinsey and his associates belong to the school I described in Chapter One, believing that values can be deduced from statistics.

The last terminological complication arises from the way in which the issue of bisexuality is currently being discussed. At the purely physical level it is indeed a universal human potential. Orgasm is a physiological response induced by physical stimulation of body parts; some people with a particuarly developed capacity for fantasy may be able to induce orgasm by merely imagining that they are being physi-

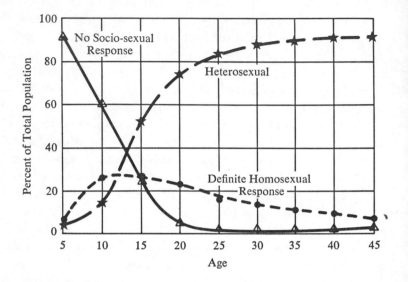

Figure 170. Development of heterosexuality and homosexuality by age periods

Active incidence curves, corrected for U. S. population. Males with no socio-sexual response (rating X) rapidly disappear between the ages of 5 and 20. Males whose responses are chiefly heterosexual (rating 0 or 1) rapidly increase in number until they ultimately account for 90 per cent of the whole population. Males who are more than incidentally homosexual in response or overt activity (ratings 2 to 6) are most abundant in pre-adolescence and through the teens, gradually becoming less abundant with advancing age.

cally stimulated, but this is relatively rare. Now the body parts in question do not know or care who or what is supplying the stimulation. After a certain point in the proceedings orgasm may occur as a purely physical result, even if the person finds the particular situation repulsive. For example, women who are being raped sometimes, to their immeasurable horror, experience orgasm on this exclusively physiological basis. Much more common, however, is the psychological inhibition of the body's sexual response when the particular social or physical circumstances of the encounter are unacceptable. It is for this reason that at the psychological level (as distinct from the purely physical level) bisexuality is most definitely not a universal human adult potential. For most people it is so unacceptable as to be impossible.

It is incorrect to describe as bisexual those persons who, while primarily homosexual, may occasionally have sexual relations with someone of the opposite sex; such acts may be undertaken either by homosexuals who have chosen marriage for social and family reasons, or during the process of transition to a heterosexual adaptation, or (and this is not uncommon) by those attempting to deny to themselves the fact of their homosexuality. I shall define the bisexual person as one who, with equal ease and pleasure, engages in sexual encounters with persons of either sex. It becomes immediately evident that what is involved here is a value judgment. Such a person perceives sex as a purely physical activity designed for the purpose of bodily pleasure. Some may prefer to engage in bisexual events only with friends and intimates, either singly or in groups, finding this type of encounter more satisfying. Others, and these are the people who go to orgies, do not require the element of relationship. Classical Freudian theory would explain such behavior as a regression to the "polymorphous perverse" stage of infantile sexuality. Now, in a climate of opinion which urges people to shed all of their sexual inhibitions in order to "realize their full sexual potential," one probably does not have to invoke the concept of primitive regression to explain all cases of bisexuality. The element of deliberate, conscious value judgment, as distinct from mainly unconscious compulsion, may now predominate in some decisions for the bisexual lifestyle. People who discover in the course of an orgy experience that they can achieve orgasm with someone of their own sex have not, contrary to popular opinion, discovered their "hitherto unrecognized homosexual potential." They have merely demonstrated that they are the kind of people whose value system permits them to go to an orgy in the first place and that the physiology of their sexual apparatus is in good working order.

There is another kind of confusion associated with contemporary uses of the term bisexuality. This has to do with the fundamentally androgynous character of the human psyche. Our culture is quite rightly involved in a widespread attempt to come to terms with this fact in a manner which will no longer involve us in massive projections of the unconscious contrasexual component onto persons of the opposite sex. When successful (as in time it surely must be), this effort will relieve us of the great social and personal burdens involved in sex role stereotyping which presently deform the lives and hinder the development of many men and women. But some writers apparently do not understand the true nature of this psychological androgyny, much less of the methods which can be useful in bringing it into effective function, and they confuse it with physical bisexuality. While there is a large amount of psychological evidence to show that real maturity brings a degree of consciousness and integration of the *animus* or *anima,* there is no evidence whatever, from any branch of the human sciences, for the idea that psychological maturity and physical bisexuality are in any way related. In fact, quite the contrary is the case. Assertions that bisexuality is a desirable and necessary concomitant of androgyny either rest on the writer's failure to distinguish the two concepts or else represent an unadorned and unsupported statement of the writer's own sexual value system. There is, naturally, nothing wrong with that—provided that it is not presented to the unwary reader as "scientific fact."[8]

Restricting the definition of homosexuality to an adult adaptation characterized by preferential sexual behavior between members of the same sex, reduces these terminological problems to manageable proportions. Some researchers, such as Dr. Charles Socarides, believe that the word "preferential" is misleading, since the subjects in question are, by virtue of their unconscious psychological conditioning, unable, rather than merely unwilling, to engage in heterosexual acts. These experts would substitute the word "obligatory" to indicate that fact. I feel that this narrows the definition excessively, since there is a significant group, certainly among men and probably also among women, who marry and have children for primarily social reasons, but whose erotic arousal and pleasure are restricted to extramarital homosexual contacts.

The statistics I cited earlier about cure refer to homosexuals thus defined. Approximately thirty percent of those coming to treatment for any reason can be converted to the heterosexual adaptation. Of course these figures cannot speak to the question of those persons whose homosexuality is relatively encapsulated in an otherwise functional personality and who therefore are less likely to seek psychiatric help. Strong motivations do sometimes cause such people to request psychotherapy in order to change their sexual orientation. Their reasons may be religious or social and may even include having formed a sufficiently deep friendship with someone of the opposite sex so that marriage could be contemplated if they were only able to engage in sexual relations. In such instances the prognosis for a successful therapeutic outcome is extremely good. This conforms to the general principle that a very well motivated individual seeking help for an isolated symptom, whose personality is otherwise intact, is always among the best candidates for successful psychotherapy or psychoanalysis.

These facts and statistics about cure are well known and not difficult to verify. In addition, there are many people who have experienced their homosexuality as a burden either for moral or social reasons who have, without the aid of psychotherapy, managed to give up this symptom; of these, a significant number have also been able to make the transition to satisfying heterosexuality. Quite apart from published studies by those who have specialized in the treatment of sexual disorders, many psychiatrists and psychologists with a more general type of practice (and I include myself in this group) have been successful in helping homosexual patients to make a complete and permanent transition to heterosexuality.

The distortion of reality inherent in the denials by homosexual apologists that the condition is curable is so immense that one wonders what motivates it. Perhaps one answer is contained in this quote from the psychologist Kurt Konietzko:

> But change is possible, and one of the problems is their resistance to that fact. The existence of one cured homosexual changes the nature of the condition in the homosexuals' eyes. It challenges them. So they try to deny it.[9]

III

---

*PROBLEMS
IN TRANSITION
FROM
"WHAT IS"
TO
"WHAT OUGHT
TO BE"*

9
The Interpretation
of Immaturity

By this time it should be evident that there is no entirely value-free way to talk about homosexuality. To begin with, there are the usual scientific problems of accurate description, definition, criteria, and standardization. I have attempted to shed some clarifying light on the conflicting reports which currently create so much confusion for the non-specialist who is responsibly trying to come to grips with the phenomenon of homosexuality as it presents itself in contemporary culture. But, in addition to these scientific questions, there is the fact that it is impossible not to have an *attitude* toward homosexuality. The lines here are clearly drawn. There are those who consider homosexuality normal and those who do not. Among those who do not, there is, and always has been, wide disagreement about just what kind of abnormality is involved. Is it only a psychiatric abnormality? Is it only a moral failure? Or is it both? The history in the West of severe disapproval, often resulting in outright persecution, is well known and need not be reviewed here. And these persecutions were often, and in some places continue to be, conducted in the very name of morality and religion. One reason for this is that the judgmental attitude which tells people they are "bad" requires far less effort than the attempt to understand people's actions so that one may responsibly and realistically help them to behave differently.

When the category of sin, currently very much out of fashion in secular and religious society, was put in limbo, people could be listened to comparatively non-judgmentally. As a result, a healing catharsis was offered to many. Without this suspension of moral judgment, there could be no scientific study of behavior. Scientists have often been naive in imagining that their own value system could be entirely set aside in the interest of objective observation and analysis of behavior. But there is no question that the responsible effort to consider the facts, all of the facts, as dispassionately as possible has resulted in a great expansion of our knowledge and understanding. Yet behind the benefits which derive from more objective examination of behavior than was possible in some former times, I see an old wolf dressed in new semantic clothing reappearing at the door. Because human nature has hardly changed at all, the word *sick* is now substituted for the word *sin*; but it carries the same subjective impact. Health is equated with virtue; social deviations are termed "neurotic," the modern equivalent of "sinful." Society, which once sent teams of missionaries and other religious professionals to police public behavior, now sends teams of psychiatrists, psychologists, and social scientists to do the same. The net effect is the same. By its hypocritical overuse of the concept of mental illness, paralleling its former misuse of the concept of sin, society attempts to control many kinds of behavior that it is unable to accept. (An extreme example of this is the political use of mental hospitalization, the modern equivalent of such religious abuses as the Inquisition.)

Such blanket condemnations have an effect precisely contrary to that which was originally intended by the creative geniuses who developed the new science of psychology. Freud and his followers, as well as those who formed new schools of their own, based their work on the humane idea that suffering individuals had to be listened to *in their own terms* before there could be any hope of ameliorating their condition. A hundred years ago it was sin that aroused indignation and caused people to withdraw disdainfully from those whom they considered to be their moral inferiors. Much of the resistance to the new psychological theories came from people who were extremely reluctant to give up their judgmental attitude toward deviance, especially when that deviance was in any way connected with sex. At that time, sickness aroused compassion and people felt moved to give tender loving care to the afflicted. The idea of having to treat with the sympathetic attention due to the sick those whom they had heretofore thought of as moral degenerates was extremely repugnant to the sensibilities of "good" people.

Consider how times have changed. The care of the sick—all sick, not just those in what the Prayer Books calls "mental darkness"—is rapidly becoming at best a profession, at worst a business, whereas in former times it was truly a vocation. It is only since World War II that anyone ever went into medicine to make a lot of money, or for purposes of upward social mobility. This change in attitude is reflected in such current phenomena as the Medicaid scandals and the outrageous rise in medical malpractice suits. I realize that there are many doctors and nurses who still approach their work in a spirit of dedicated devotion to the sick and with a full appreciation of the sacredness of the mysteries of life and death. Nevertheless, there is a general darkening of the atmosphere surrounding the care of the ill which must be causing the shades of Aesculapius, Hippocrates and St. Luke to weep. If you doubt this, consider the disgusted tone of voice in which you or someone you know has said about some particularly objectionable behavior "That's sick!" We are all guilty.

Individual sufferers, instead of being taken seriously, are now too often heard only as the discordant note in an orchestration of elaborate "scientific" interpretations. It is hardly surprising that homosexuals, feeling downgraded and devalued, resist the appellation "sick." However, both logic and common sense suggest that when a concept is being abused, as in some quarters the concept of sickness most certainly now is, the thing to do is to reform it, not to abolish it. Phenomena remain and tend to be consistent with human nature regardless of what label-changing we may engage in, either for good reasons or bad. And individuals or groups who, for whatever reasons, have a low self-image are always at least partially motivated to put the blame elsewhere. Sometimes they are right—the sad story of oppression and injustice goes back to the Fall; it is as old as the history of humanity. Sometimes, however, they are wrong. Sometimes the only way to change things is to withdraw the projections, stop blaming others for one's difficulties, and take responsibility for one's own situation and for one's own behavior. And, of course, there are times when effective change requires a combination of these two approaches.

The problem of homosexuality is clearly in this last category. It is unquestionably time for society to stop oppressing homosexuals by abrogating their civil rights and labeling their behavior criminal. (I do not speak here of those who molest children or attempt to seduce minors, or engage in violence. Such behavior is in a different category, not related to homosexuality as such, since heterosexuals commit similar offenses.) Furthermore, they must not be oppressed by those misuses of the concept of illness which perpetuate their second-class citizenship. But it is also time for homosexuals to stop shouting "Oppressor!" at anyone who dares to say that homosexuality is less than normal.

I believe the underlying problematic issue is that of responsibility. The average educated person today, brought up in an intellectual climate permeated by popularized and diluted versions of Freudian theory, believes that psychoanalysis states that people are not responsible for their neuroses because these are caused by unconscious complexes, the result of infantile or childhood trauma over which they have no control. This oversimplification, while it contains some truth, does violence to a central aspect of Freud's theory. There is a crucial distinction between *trauma* and *conflict.* In a brilliant article discussing the impact of modern sex research on psychoanalytic thought, Dr. Robert Stoller, a distinguished professor of psychiatry who has specialized in the study and treatment of sexual deviation, explains the difference. Trauma may be in the form of internal sensations, such as hunger or pain; or it may be in the form of external events, such as physical violence or the death of a parent. Such trauma may only cause reaction or change. The affected infant or child may, with more or less pain, automatically adapt to the new circumstances. Dr. Stoller goes on to say that "Not all [traumas] produce conflict; conflict implies intrapsychic struggle in order to *choose* among possibilities."[1]

It is conflict, not trauma, which produces an internal fork in the developmental road. The reason this is so important is that neuroses, including perversion of the sexual development, do not result simply from trauma, but from particular resolutions of conflict in this technical sense of that word. As a result of conflict the individual *chooses,* however primitively and unconsciously, one solution over another. It seems to be this element of choice which is so antagonistic to the modern consciousness and which most modern sex research opposes. Dr. Stoller describes this as follows:

> The new research seems aimed unanimously at tearing down the conflict theory; no other aspect of Freud's system has created such resistance, perhaps because Freud believed perversion is *motivated,* i. e., that a person is somehow, in his depths, in part responsible for his perversion. The deviant act, Freud felt, is the product of the great human capacity for choice and so ultimately has a moral quality (even if one's responsibility is mitigated because the choice is unconscious and was arrived at because of unsought threatening circumstances in childhood).[2]

The attack on the conflict theory has taken four forms, each of which attempts to substitute a morally neutral explanation of the behavior. The first of these alternate theories proposes that all manner of deviant sexual behavior is to be explained in terms of purely physiological mechanisms, including genetic predisposition. The second main school postulates conditioning mechanisms as the exclusive or principal cause of sexual deviance. In this view human beings are seen as mere collections of reflexes, however elaborate and sophisticated; everything we do is either to secure pleasure or to avoid pain, and the correction of undesired behavior is to be achieved by the deliberate substitution of a more efficient set of reflexes for the old ones which were not working to the subject's advantage. The third attack on Freud's conflict theory attempts to substitute statistical explanations. Here it is asserted that there is a distribution curve for the various forms of sexual behavior. Deviance from the norm is not seen as abnormal—it is merely unusual. Finally there are those who believe that the many differing ways in which various forms of sexual behavior have been valued is entirely explainable according to the principle of cultural relativity. Nothing is intrinsically abnormal, although it may be so labeled as a result of the sexual taboos of a particular culture. Those who favor this explanation may add that while the behavior itself is not sick, cultural condemnation of it is.

All four of these explanations are being urged in the specific case of homosexuality, and homosexual apologists draw heavily on them in their own presentations. The Church, which has more than a little reason to have collective guilt feelings because of its contribution to the climate of unjust persecution which homosexuals have had to endure, may be peculiarly vulnerable to acceptance of the last argument, that of cultural relativity. Dr. Stoller's interpretation of the significance of all of these views is this:

> . . . the author uses the research of others to support his position for sexual freedom. This is especially the case with activists banded together to relieve the guilt and social degradation traditionally laid upon them. Homosexuals exemplify this approach . . .[Here the four attacks on conflict theory are summarized] . . . *Crucial for each of these defenses is the relief of guilt: since one's self did not choose it, one is not responsible for it, and besides the condition is not shameful.* [3]

He concludes this discussion with the following extremely significant observation: "We may not solve these moral issues, which masquerade as scientific ones, as easily as each side hopes." Human behavior unavoidably stands between *what is* and *what ought to be,* and any examination of it must therefore involve us not only in scientific but also in moral reflection. To try to avoid such issues merely compounds problems into the future and is therefore irresponsible. As Dr. Stoller says, these questions cannot be answered easily. Nevertheless, the effort to address them must be made; perhaps that difficult task can be eased by attempting to separate the moral from the scientific components.

It has been conclusively demonstrated that there is a usual progression from infancy to maturity which involves many different steps of psycho-social development. I have already described the principal ways in which the homosexual adaptation involves a failure to take one or more of these steps. In this sense, homosexuality is immature. I have tried unsuccessfully to find some word other than *immature* because this, too, has a "bad" connotation. And therein lies the question: should the failure to take all the possible maturational steps be assigned a moral value? In a later chapter I shall discuss that question in more detail. But first, some closer scrutiny of the nature of immaturity must be undertaken.

It is interesting to compare the descriptions of homosexual behavior and dynamics as given by homosexual apologists with the descriptions by those holding the view that it is deviant. In *The Ego in Love and Sexuality,* Dr. Edrita Fried writes:

> The inadequately developed ego resembles an old-fashioned and ill-equipped workshop. Certain tools are missing altogether, because the mind, having developed in an unhealthy and discouraging setting, has not been guided to develop them. Other tools are outmoded and should be replaced by up-to-date equipment. . . . The inadequately developed mind, like the inadequately equipped tool shop, can deal only with selected tasks. It is, in particular, not prepared to cope with the powerful physiological and psychological challenges of love and sexuality.[4]

In the section on homosexuality she describes nearly all the same behavior described by Tripp, sometimes in identical language. Particularly striking is the comparison of his description of "male bonding" with hers of the "homosexual collective." She notes the similarity to adolescent groups which are a means to strength needed by the immature. He gives exactly the same reason—but without the loaded label "immature." What she calls regression he glorifies; he simply denies that there is anything wrong with it. (To all psychologists, even Tripp, "regression" is a pejorative term.)

As we have seen, Tripp considers agression and hostility central to eroticism, including its heterosexual varieties. Fried, by contrast, perceives sexual hostility as a defense against the mature heterosexual experience of fusion or union with the partner. To those who are inadequately prepared for it, this can be very unsettling. One romantic

Frenchman has described orgasm as "le petit mort"—"the little death." This dramatic phrase expresses the frightening aspect of the psychological experience of the dissolution of the boundaries of the personal ego which attends full expression of sexual feeling. The old Biblical language describes this, not as something to fear, but as an ideal: "They two shall become one flesh." But to people who are insecure in their own identity, who fear that if they really let themselves go they may not be able to find themselves again, such intimate union may evoke powerful inhibitions and defense mechanisms. Hostility clearly establishes that "you are you, and I am I, and the way I know this for sure is because we are fighting; because I am so busy creating distance between us I cannot possibly lose myself in my experience of you." It is only through some such unconscious line of reasoning that many people are able to permit themselves to enjoy the occasional fleeting pleasures of physiological orgasm. Real closeness sustained over time in a relationship is too threatening to their precarious psychological organization. Both Drs. Fried and Tripp proclaim the presence of hostility in certain kinds of sexual response; they simply value it differently. She sees it as an immature technique to stave off intimacy; he sees it as a necessary and desirable support to self-centered autonomy, and goes on to make the preposterous claim that such unfortunate arrested development is universal.

The whole issue of the valuation of maturity is widespread in our culture, and the new permissive terms in which homosexuality is being discussed may well be only one instance, possibly even a consequence, of a more general trend. In his review of Benjamin Spock's recent book, *Raising Children in a Difficult Time,* Irving Kristol makes the following observations:

> If Dr. Spock is to be faulted—and I think he is—it is not because he gives bad advice about how to cope with children, but because he has helped promote a flawed conception of adulthood.

Kristol perceives Spock's values to be "off" in these ways:

Freudianism without frustration, socialism without coercion . . . a kind of adolescent political fantasy in which the good things in life are available without cost . . . values which assure them that it is only authority which deforms life and that the absence of authority will liberate us all toward perfect happiness. The consequence is that they never truly become adults themselves . . . they can propose to their children no honorable model of adulthood. . . . The result is the worldwide shortage of adults and the surplus of "kids" that we are now experiencing.[5]

The artist is often a prophet; today we are seeing the new and sinister meaning of James M. Barrie's "delightful" *Peter Pan*—the immature boy-girl lost in hedonistic fantasy, the carefree innocence exposed as a destructive refusal to accept the terror or the ecstasy of adult responsibility.

These reflections will be seen to complement the discussion in Chapter Seven of those problems which result from inappropriate perpetuation of the maternal tie. It is significant that Dr. Spock's famous first book was the child-care bible for millions of young women engaged in the pathetic attempt to become super-mothers in the period following World War II.

Alan Jones, a professor of ethics at an Episcopal theological seminary, connects homosexuality with immaturity in still another way. He writes:

There is a danger of our defining our humanity solely in sexual terms. . . . When someone admits to being one or the other [homosexual or heterosexual] my first reaction is to ask, "Is that all? Are you anything more? Do you define yourself solely in terms of what you imagine to be your sexual preference?". . . To my mind no one should announce their sexual identity until they are well over thirty and then do so, if they must, very *quietly.*[6]

Of course he is right—ideally. But a full understanding of the maturational progression involved in homosexuality makes clear why the contemporary scene is different. Just as only the rich can afford the luxury of believing that it is vulgar to discuss money, so only the truly mature are entirely able to consider their identity apart from sex. Therefore, the less mature people are, the more unsolicited information we may expect to hear from them about their sex life. And the more insecure (either emotionally or morally) they are about what they are doing, the more we may expect to hear either a defensive or aggressive note in their insistence that it is "all right," and the more we may expect them to ally vociferously with others who are engaging in the same behavior. Parents who have watched over a youngster on the painful path through adolescent sexual awakening and value formation will surely recognize this picture.

For mature people, however, Father Jones is right. Unless pushed by some overriding social necessity, mature people tend not to discuss their sex life as such. This may explain why we hear so much about immature sexuality, heterosexual as well as homosexual, and so little that is really specific or descriptive about sex that is truly grown-up. There are few models for mature sexuality in culture or literature, which is another reason why family influence is so important. Unless people have the fortunate experience of being raised by two parents who really care about one another as adult men and women, they are not likely to have the opportunity to learn much about how sexuality works in a mature context.

Art tends to take up the failures, not the successes. This may be because failure is considered more interesting, more dramatic; in Tolstoi's words, "All happy families are alike." Far from believing that statement, which has been uncritically accepted as clear and profound truth, I think it is an exceptionally dangerous and destructive lie. It proposes that happiness is boring, predictable, monotonous. This is not unlike the static perfection of the old pictures of heaven in which everyone sits on a cloud playing a harp forever. No eating and drinking, certainly no sex, no stimulating conversation or challenge because everyone always agrees with everyone else about everything, nothing to stir the blood, not even any really interesting music. Who needs it? How much more enticing are the artistic visions of tragedy!

In Xanadu did Kubla Khan
A stately pleasure-dome decree:
Where Alph, the sacred river, ran
Through caverns measureless to man
Down to a sunless sea.

. . .

A savage place! as holy and enchanted
As e'er beneath a waning moon was haunted
By woman wailing for her demon-lover![7]

That example from Coleridge taken together with our insipid picture of heaven makes vivid the contrast between our ability to be articulate about unhappiness and our nearly complete inability to be articulate about happiness. Our efforts to do the latter have a regrettable tendency to deteriorate into sentimentality supported by a platform of clichés. Much sex education suffers from this defect when it attempts to go beyond an equally inadequate and misleading focus on the purely physical aspects.

The fact that it is so difficult to describe does not mean that true happiness does not exist—and in an infinite profusion of vivid and life-supporting forms. I believe that happy families do not easily yield the secret sources and subtle qualities of their happiness—not because they don't want to, but because it is so difficult. The more developed people are (and development here is not to be confused with mere education or with cosmopolitan sophistication), the less they are fixated at the purely material or physical levels of existence. Their happiness has far less to do with *what* they do—which, to the outsider, may even seem dull—but with *how* they do it, with what it *means* to them, and with its spiritual place in the fabric of their relationships and the total context of their life. Nor can this be taught by purely educational techniques since these are mainly effective in conveying those lessons which can be apprehended through our rational faculties. Feeling and intuition must be nourished in a prolonged matrix of experience.

Perhaps an example may illustrate this point, at least through a glass darkly. It is quite possible to teach people the techniques of nutrition and cooking by the use of cookbooks and demonstration classes. It is not possible to teach them by these means how to enjoy their food, or to appreciate the subtleties of esthetic meal planning, much less to teach them how to go on from there to exercise their own creativity in the culinary art. Great cooks are almost never able to explain or convey the subtle factors which differentiate them from the merely competent ones. A memorable meal involves all who prepare it far beyond the limits of mere skill and all who partake of it in satisfaction far beyond the limits of mere taste. The only cookbook I know which even attempts to deal with this issue is Robert Capon's *Supper of the Lamb,* and in order to do so the author had to resort to theological categories.[8]

To try to explain why mature people tend not to talk about their sex life, you will notice that I had to stop talking about sex as such. At the upper levels of human development it is simply irrelevant *as such,* but paradoxically becomes infinitely more significant and precious to those who do engage in it. Since the whole person, spirit and mind as well as emotions and body, is in union with the whole person of the partner, there is no way to consider the sexual aspects of the encounter separately without doing violence to its nature and distorting the true character of the experience beyond all recognition. In addition to being an important reason why we hear so little about truly mature heterosexuality, this may help to explain why the "well-adjusted, healthy" homosexual is also so difficult to find. Precisely to the extent that homosexual adaptation is a nearly isolated pocket of developmental failure in a person whose other qualities are very well-developed—precisely to that extent are such homosexuals likely to be silent about their condition.

However, under the pressure of contemporary discussion of the issue, some responsible homosexuals have spoken out. In welcome contrast to the hostile immaturities of Tripp's book, consider this passage from a distinguished professor of theology, Norman Pittenger:

Who is to establish what is truly normal for men and women? In my own view, it is normal for them to express their sexuality in a desire to love another of their race through mutual giving and receiving, through as much personal relationship as is possible, and through a concern for others in every area of their personhood. And it is abnormal to hate, to be cruel and hurtful, to treat persons as things, to act irresponsibly toward them and with them. To act in this latter fashion is indeed deviant; it is to act subhumanly and to violate the very nature of the love toward which men are meant to be moving.[9]

Without agreeing with his implication that homosexuality *per se* is normal, one can certainly respect his general approach to the standards which ought to be applied to human relatedness; nor can one doubt that these standards point in the direction of maturity.

The complete self-absorption of infancy precludes an awareness of the existence of others, to say nothing of the fact that those others are separate selves with needs of their own. The socialization and acculturation processes which bring us from this beginning even to a relative state of maturity are so diverse and complex as to defy complete analysis. No one ever arrives at the goal in every particular—in fact, the psychological growth process can continue into advanced old age, if only along some parameters. Most of us, however, have at least a few complexes, the result of infantile or childhood conflicts which we are unable to eradicate and which manifest themselves as particular areas of immaturity which persist into our adult lives. Another cause of pockets of adult immaturity is the failure to actualize some potential because the environmental stimuli required to encourage its flowering were absent.

Because of the biological givenness of our maleness or femaleness, sexuality and personhood are inextricably linked. This means that the general maturation process inevitably affects and is affected by the more narrowly defined development of sexual attitudes, preference and behavior. It is for this reason that any thorough and sustained course of self-examination, be this conducted under the rubric of psychotherapy, spiritual direction, programs of meditation (secular or religious), or any other theoretical framework, sooner or later involves the subjects in some consideration of their sexuality. It is for this reason that no description or discussion of maturity can be complete without the processes of observation, discernment and evaluation being directed toward the sexual as well as all other aspects of growth and development; furthermore, the way in which these are inter-related must also be examined.

Recognizing that the goal can never be fully or consistently real-ized, I shall describe the mature state as that in which one is so confident of one's own identity and worth that one can give freely without feeling diminished, and receive without a sense of anxious obligation. Furthermore, one has developed one's perceptions of inter-nal as well as external reality and one's intellectual and moral assess-ments of those realities to the point where one can make honest mistakes without a crippling sense of guilt, and can enjoy one's suc-cesses without the distortion of pride. A profound sense of responsibil-ity, both to oneself and to others, can be expected to flow naturally from those who have made significant progress along the road to such a goal. (You will notice that in spite of its ultimate unattainability, perfection is not part of this description.)

Until recently it would not have been necessary to defend publicly for a serious audience the idea that progress to maturity, however defined, is desirable. Typical of those now questioning this once self-evident ideal is Norman O. Brown. In such books as *Life Against Death* and *Love's Body* he has taken the view that all maturity is purchased at the unacceptable price of freedom. He accepts Freud's views about the primacy of the sexual instinct and that only by repression of its development and manifestations can "progress" take place. He sees this process as unavoidably accompanied by frustration and misery and goes on to extol the virtues of return to the infantile state of "polymorphous perverse sexuality" where all could be lost in a Dionysian ecstasy of instinctual gratification. But recently, when asked why he himself did not adopt such a lifestyle, his reply was: "Because then I wouldn't be able to write!"

10
The Goals of Human Sexuality

I will make your descendants like the dust on the ground: when men succeed in counting the specks of dust on the ground, then they will be able to count your descendants!
Genesis 13:16

Look up to heaven and count the stars if you can. Such will be your descendants.
Genesis 15:15

The population explosion of the twentieth century, coupled with the dawning realization that the natural resources of the world are not inexhaustible and that famine now threatens to become the leading cause of death for millions of men, women and children, make the ancient promises quoted above sound rather like prophecies of terrible doom. But until very recently, no greater assurance of successful competition in the battle of life could possibly have been offered. It is only since World War I that the transition from an agricultural to an industrial society has been fully accomplished in the developed nations of the West. This same time span has also seen the flowering of modern medicine. These two developments have radically altered the external realities which affect our attitudes toward reproduction.

In agricultural society, before the invention of sophisticated farm machinery and when each farm was a family business, the more children you had, the more food you could produce. In fact, the pattern of school vacations which we take for granted and which persists to this day reflects that fact. The spring vacation was designed to permit the children to work during the planting season and the long summer vacation permitted their essential presence in the fields. Even the smallest children, girls as well as boys, were pressed into service to tend and harvest the crops or care for the animals. Since everything was done with only the simplest tools, either wielded by hand or horse-drawn, many unpaid workers were required if the farm was to be a financial success. This pattern was essentially unchanged since the time of Abraham, to whom the ancient promises at the beginning of this chapter were made, and a large family was therefore truly a blessing.

At the same time, owing to the very high infant and childhood mortality rate, it was not easy to raise a large family to maturity. Readers old enough to remember the time before the discovery of antibiotics will recall the practice of quarantining not only the victims but the families of those stricken with such maladies as diphtheria, scarlet fever and whooping cough in an attempt to fend off the spread of these highly contagious and frequently fatal diseases. Most living Americans have been moved to special compassion for Rose Kennedy because of the untimely death of four out of her nine children. But we must remember that only three or four generations ago it was commonplace for women to lose such a proportion of their children, although disease rather than violence was the usual cause. In these circumstances the bearing of many children was, in addition to its other advantages, an assurance of bringing a reasonable number of them to maturity.

We have also lost sight of the fact that until relatively recent times —in fact, within the memory of some now living—childbirth was fraught with peril for the mother as well as the infant. Indeed, only a few generations ago women having their babies by Caesarian section might well have died in labor. But beyond the difficulties of the birth process itself, untold numbers of women formerly succumbed to puerperal sepsis, commonly known as "childbed fever." An afternoon spent perusing the inscriptions on tombstones in an old cemetery will vividly point up the fact that in the course of siring an economically rewarding number of offspring, a Colonial or early Victorian patriarch not only lost a goodly number of infants and children to disease, but frequently went through two or three wives as well. Effective and safe methods of birth control had yet to be discovered. Under these economic and medical conditions, the reproductive goal of human sexuality was so inescapable and so obviously advantageous that it was never seriously questioned.

If sense is to be made of the official utterances of both Scripture and theological tradition over the centuries, and of the common moral standards which resulted, it is extremely important to understand the realities of the cultural conditions prevailing at the time the statements were made. Most people in our urban, technological society have a disproportionate sense of the contemporary and almost no sense of history or of nature. But the hostile contempt which the majority of modern writers heap on the standards of previous eras is usually grounded in a profound ignorance of the realities of daily life which were the matrix of those standards. To take just one example, it is now fashionable to cite the ancient custom of considering women "unclean" for several weeks after childbirth as evidence of nothing more than patriarchal oppression designed to underscore and enforce female inferiority. What is forgotten is that knowledge of the connection between standards of cleanliness and hygiene and the incidence and spread of disease is now *only one hundred years old;* before then people seldom bathed, bed linen and bandages were infrequently changed, there were no antibiotics or antiseptics, wounds were not cleaned, doctors did not wash their hands between patients, and septicemia (blood poisoning) was a leading cause of death. Childbirth is, at best, impressively messy. Before the germ theory and modern sanitation, it was not realized that to clear away that mess immediately was, quite literally, a matter of life and death. The new mother was really, not just metaphorically, unclean and a potential focus of fatal infection, both to herself and to others.

I do not, of course, mean to imply that more abstract social attitudes were not also at work in the formation and continuation of the ancient customs of ritual female uncleanness, as well as in all the other regulations bearing upon sexual customs and behavior. But the predominantly masculine approaches to history which focus on the study of power and aggression (kings and conquest, dates and battles) or on the "history of ideas" (as though ideas had a separate, disembodied existence) do not provide us with that vivid sense of practical problems and immediate texture and flavor of daily life without which intelligent understanding of the past is impossible.

Before the Industrial Revolution it would not have occurred to anyone to question the essential reproductive goal of human sexuality; in fact, such a question could only have been put in the context of hedonistic avoidance of reproductive responsibility. Gradually, as the shift from agricultural to industrial social organization got under way, and as Malthus and others began to consider the problem of feeding an expanding urban population, it became clear that large families were no longer always advantageous. One input into the (from our vantage point) anti-sexual attitudes of the last century was just this attempt to control family size. Reliable methods of birth control had not yet been discovered. It must also be remembered that, comparatively speaking, very little was known about reproductive physiology and there was great reluctance to tamper with the mysterious natural processes. This reluctance was reinforced by the fact that practically nothing was known about heredity; not only could the immediate consequences of interference with the reproductive process not be surely foreseen, but it was feared that more remote consequences for future generations might possibly be harmful.

Typical of much that was written at the time is a book by Mrs. Emma F. Angell Drake, M. D., *What Every Young Wife Ought To Know*, published in 1908. Throughout the whole book it is clear how difficult it was at that time to deal with the practical problem of limiting family size without also putting strong moral limits on the exercise of natural sexual desire. For example, in a chapter entitled "The Marital Relations—The Subject Approached with Reluctance" we find such passages as the following:

Be guarded, O husband! It is a woman's nature to forgive, and when she loves, this impetuosity of passion uncontrolled, can be many times forgiven. Aye, even when too frequent maternity is thrust upon her; but there comes a time when love and forgiveness have reached their limit, and love struggles vainly to rise above disgust and loathing, but it can never again attain to anything but tolerance.[1]

(Those tempted to read into this passage nothing but a denial of female sexuality should remember not only the facts about the past presented earlier in this chapter, but also how frequently modern psychoanalytic therapy finds fear of pregnancy in cases of frigidity, even though this fear is nowadays seldom based on medical anxiety about the birth process.) Later in the chapter Dr. Drake goes on to say ". . . that there should be no pandering to sexual indulgence, while there is unwillingness to bear as many children as a proper manly and womanly Christian temperance in these things will allow."[2] It is clear that even though the need to limit family size was recognized, the idea of questioning reproduction as the central goal of sex relations was not yet seen as contributing to anything but lust, in contrast to true love. (The very word *lust* is now out of fashion, but the outraged energy with which even the most secular feminists complain about being treated as "sex objects" suggests that it may have been abandoned prematurely.)

The consciousness of reproduction as the central goal appears to have contributed heavily to the view that sexual acts other than coitus itself were perverse. Throughout much of the United States there remain on the books to this day laws forbidding oral-genital contact even between married couples. Masturbation, also condemned, was formerly known as onanism; this derives from the story in Genesis 38:8–10 of Onan, who "spilled his seed on the ground" for which he was slain by Yahweh. However, it is clear that the offense was not masturbation as such, but Onan's refusal to impregnate his dead brother's wife according to Jewish law. In fact, it is impossible to be sure from the actual wording of the text whether Onan's avoidance of his reproductive responsibility was achieved by masturbation or by coitus interruptus.

While it is true that our forbears never lost sight of their inevitable procreative duty, it is equally true that this was never the only consideration applied to the evaluation of various forms of sexual behavior. In our liberal, not to say libertine, age it is fashionable to quote only those spokesmen of bygone times who have seen sex chiefly as a deplorable necessity which exposed its participants to the twin dangers of sin and madness. At no time in history was such a view truly predominant or actually constitutive of the real belief and practice of ordinary people. Professor Singer's book, *The Goals of Human Sexuality,* contains the best review I have seen of the history of this issue. Particularly illuminating is his discussion of the various ways of considering it which have prevailed through Christian history. An important distinction which he clarifies is between the sensuous and the passionate attitude to sexual behavior; he demonstrates that religious and moral authorities have taken differing stances to these two components of sexuality. Furthermore, the stances taken have varied from one era to another, there being a fairly clear tendency to approve one approach while condemning the other.

An amusing illustration of this point is provided by a story from the Middle Ages, related in a derisively satirical tone by Bertrand Russell. A priest inquires whether it is sinful for him to fondle the breasts of a nun during confession and is told by his superiors that it is not, provided that he does so "without evil intent." Clearly this incident took place in an age which approved the sensuous while deploring the passionate. Professor Singer convincingly demonstrates that the Victorian period favored passion at the expense of sensuousness, which goes far to explain why much writing of the time deplored or actually condemned much sexual foreplay. At the present time the pendulum has swung again, and we are unquestionably living in a sensuous era. Generally speaking, it is probably true that the sexual needs of women are best served in predominantly sensuous rather than exclusively passionate atmospheres. This is not, however, as true as most people suppose, which may in part account for the fact that current research into women's sexual fantasies shows a significant rise in images of being dominated by the male, often including fantasies of actual rape. It is inarguable that happily mated couples through the centuries, regardless of sexual standards publicly endorsed by the culture, have found and practiced their own personally satisfying blend of the two styles.

It has been said that those who do not learn from history are condemned to repeat it. There has never been a society which did not have some important rules governing sexual behavior. If we persist in the present trend to overthrow all of our own Western sexual heritage

in the name of "liberation," without truly understanding the significance of that which we are so hastily discarding, we run the serious
risk of undercutting aspects of our culture which we can ill afford to
do without. There are now many who do not know how to discern
the difference between oppression and discipline. It is equally important to retain the distinction between freedom and license. Much
popular contemporary rhetoric (and some not so popular, from the
pen of those who ought to know better) would have us believe that
our ancestors were engaged in mindless reproduction on the one hand,
and sinister repression of sexual pleasure on the other. Words like
"puritanical" and "Victorian" have become no more than unflattering
epithets used to dismiss out of hand attitudes considered too antique
to require serious examination. However, in another part of their
compartmentalized minds these same authors may admire the forti-
tude, independence and ingenuity of the early Puritan settlers of New
England, the political sophistication of the Victorian statesmen who
brought constitutional monarchy to full flower, and the intellectual
brilliance of Victorian scientists such as Darwin, Huxley and Ruther-
ford. It never seems to occur to these "thinkers" that there might be
a connection between these phenomena. The clear lesson of history is
that cultural customs, including sexual morés, are never divorced
from the political, social and intellectual development of an era. As
J. L. Cameron expresses it, ". . . in the past, modes of sexual behavior
have been one thread in the web of culture, and the pattern and
integrity of the web depend upon the disposition of every thread."[3]

The placement of the sexual thread in culture's web has always been
dependent upon the answers to three questions. What is sex for? Who
may engage in it, and with whom? What sexual acts are permissible
and under what circumstances?

I believe it is demonstrable that the answers to the second and third
of these questions have always been contingent upon the answer to
the first. It is true that, at various times in history—and by no means
only Christian history—some have tried to claim that sex was *only*
for reproduction. From the purely religious point of view, such a
claim is a grave heresy; from the psychiatric point of view it is demon-

strably false. That sex is pleasurable has always been known and, for the most part, thoroughly appreciated. Sometimes the pleasure has been seen as dangerous, tending to precipitate people into the temptations of lust. Others have seen the pleasure as providing a most necessary cement to the otherwise fragile covenant of marriage. Still others have perceived sexual pleasure as an essential precondition of the responsible business of reproduction, for without such enticement people would probably never do anything so intrinsically ludicrous and peculiar! Throughout the many variations on these and other themes, nobody until the present century ever seriously questioned that the *primary* answer to the question "What is sex for?" was the reproduction of the human species.

One set of answers to the second and third questions is obviously contingent on this fact. The restriction of sexual partnership to those situations providing for the orderly devolution of lineage and property, assuring the nurture and training of children, and protecting the species against the perils of inbreeding, clearly supports the reproductive purpose. Promiscuity, incest, and homosexuality could be understandably proscribed for this reason alone; even within marriage, non-coital acts engaged in as a substitute for (rather than as a prelude to) coitus and the practice of birth control have also been prohibited on these same grounds. These marital prohibitions can be shown to rest on too narrow an interpretation of reproductive purpose, but are, nevertheless, indissolubly connected with it.

Now in the last quarter of the twentieth century we have reached a new point in human history. Not only do we realize that it is no longer desirable that reproduction should be the primary goal of sex, but we have also developed reliable methods of birth control so that, for the first time, it is possible to avoid reproduction safely without resorting to sexual abstinence. The full impact of these changes has yet to be appreciated. I know of no congress of theologians or secular ethicists which has gathered for serious debate of the new question: if the primary goal and consequence of sex is no longer reproduction, *what is it?*

The failure of responsible professionals to engage this issue directly has left a vacuum in our culture and the result has been a rapid removal of sex from the area of ethical and moral concern. Nearly all behavioral scientists, and a deplorably large number of theologians and other ethical "experts" desperate to climb onto the contemporary bandwagon in order to appear liberal, relevant, and "with it," have unthinkingly accepted this pseudo-scientific position. Those who have tried to resist have been shouted down with such epithets as "intellectual troglodyte," "prude," "guilt-monger," and many more. But it seems to me that only in a relentlessly reductionistic culture which tries to explain everything in terms of its simplest components, preferably physical or at least primitively instinctual, could such a situation have come about. The idea that the primary goal of human sexuality is the pleasurable reduction of instinctual tension, surrounded by whatever sophisticated elaborations or props individuals may find enhancing, could only be accepted in a culture such as ours without being seriously questioned.

In a recent issue of the *New York Review of Books,* J. M. Cameron discusses seven contemporary books about sex, two of them by religious professionals, and finds them all sadly lacking in any sense of the moral issues. He writes:

> It is very common now for people to find such a [moral] discussion boring and stupid. They are confident there is a hedonistic calculus that will get them out of their moral difficulties and they have a strong impression that somehow or other it has been shown, to all except a few religious freaks, that all moral requirements "exist by people thinking this or that" . . . in the works so far discussed there is no serious consideration of the moral problems that may be raised by changes in the sexual mores of our society; still less is the notion ever canvassed of the possibility of there being in this field absolute interdictions. Very occasionally, perhaps, this is discussed, but with derision, as modern chemists would talk about phlogiston. . . .
> Free sexual activity seems at first glance to offer a happy corner where all is sweetness and light. A second or a third glance leaves one a bit unsure. . . .

After dismissing the book by Eugene Bianchi and Rosemary Ruether and the one by Father Richard Ginder with the words "Their standards of argument are poor and their understanding of history is defective," he goes on to deplore the fact that there is no feeling for the immensely old human tradition of venerating the powers of sexuality and hedging them about with taboos, myths, piety; an attitude for which the sexual is not an extra, a relaxation, a consolation, a relief of tension, though it may also be all these things, but a part of the sacred order of the cosmos. . . .

In the end the indictment of liberated sexuality . . . is that it makes sex trivial and empties life of its difficult mystery.[4]

A culture which prides itself on its devotion to knowledge cannot afford to continue to deal with so crucial an issue as sex in the shallow way which currently prevails. Nothing we know from history, anthropology, or any other discipline supports the idea of sex as *only* a pleasurable activity, any more than as *only* a reproductive one. Sex is not just a technique for "getting closer to those you love," for instance. Who is to say that getting closer, however pleasurable that may be, is always a desideratum? Or that the means do not matter? Or that one way is as loving as another?

These questions must all be examined seriously. It must be ascertained whether there are any goals to human sexuality beyond the physical ones of reproduction and pleasure. If sex is found to have some serious symbolic significance, the nature of this might well have a bearing on the moral implications of homosexuality.

IV

"WHAT OUGHT TO BE"— SOME THEOLOGICAL REFLECTIONS

11
The Moral Significance
of Immaturity

*I*n Chapter Nine, an important question emerged, one which is ultimately theological, not scientific. Should the failure to take all possible maturational steps be assigned a moral value? If so, how can religious people decide the application of this principle to homosexuality? Odd as it might at first appear, I believe that the wholesale rejection of Christianity which we see in the rising forces of secularization is due to exactly the same reason that there is the strong current attack on classic psychoanalytic theory. It consists in the rejection of the idea of real personal responsibility. Dr. Stoller's discussion of Freudian conflict theory pointed out that the reason the theory is under such intense attack is because it insists that *all conduct, even when the motivations are unconscious, is the result of choice, and that therefore people are ultimately responsible in their depths.* In fact, upon closer examination it is clear that were this not true, psychotherapy could not possibly ever work. People cannot change that which is entirely beyond their control. The process of psychotherapy entails a very large element of helping sufferers to understand that they are *not* victims of something beyond themselves, but that choices made in the past, however unconsciously, can be reviewed and new decisions taken.

Any system of therapy which does not start with this premise is ultimately manipulative in character, resting on behaviorist and materialistic assumptions which view the human being as a collection of elaborate reflexes and conditionings. There is no moral dimension to such treatment. It can provide no base for the development of a firm, independent value system in the patient. This is because all symptoms, all forms of distress, are perceived, not as the consequences of the sufferer having *acted* in particular ways, but rather of the sufferer having *been acted upon,* either by internal or external forces. Treatment does not involve developing the faculty of decision informed by feeling and intellect, but in *acting upon* the patient in such a way that the unpleasant effects of the distressing conditions are obviated. Suffering is perceived only as something to be gotten rid of at all costs, and as quickly as possible. The patient is to be "reprogrammed" (the body is only a fancy computer, after all) not to react with anxiety or emotional pain to stimuli which were formerly disturbing.

The difficulty with this approach is subtle, but of far-reaching importance. A comparison with physical medicine may make the point. Bodily pain is a sign that there is something wrong; if such pain is more than mild and transient a physican should be consulted. The doctor understands that the pain itself is not the problem, but only a sign which points to the problem. After suitable diagnostic procedures which in themselves may sometimes be lengthy and painful, a treatment program is prescribed to eliminate the cause of the pain. The use of pain-killers is justified only in two circumstances: after diagnostic procedures have been completed, in order to make the patient comfortable during the treatment program; or as a compassionate palliative measure in those cases where it has been established that there is no hope of real cure. A physician whose therapeutic technique consisted only in getting rid of pain without investigating and treating the fundamental causes of it would quickly be recognized as a dangerous fool.

In an analogous way, anxiety, depression, and the other forms of psychological pain and disturbed behavior which lead distressed people to seek professional help are only signs that something is wrong. These symptoms are not, in and of themselves, constitutive of what is wrong. The damage done to people by applying the therapeutic techniques designed to get rid of symptoms, without any attempt at understanding the true nature of the underlying problems which gave rise to them, can be very great indeed. It leaves them in the existential position of being a victim of circumstances, whether these be internal or external—usually, of course, some dialectical combination of both. The corollary is that they are not assisted to take any real responsibility for their own situation. Some people, therapists as well as patients, welcome this position since it obviates what is perceived as an unnecessary burden of guilt for past errors in judgment. This is a dangerous oversimplification. There are far worse things than guilt: in particular, the loss of freedom which inevitably accompanies the refusal to take appropriate responsibility.

Freedom and responsibility go hand in hand and come in roughly equal increments. The attempt to enjoy one without the other always leads to trouble. It is possible to describe the Victorian era as one which laid too much stress on responsibility at the expense of freedom, and a corrective move toward liberation from that strain was inevitable. In our time, the pendulum has swung dangerously far in the other direction. Systems of dealing with human suffering which do not go beyond the attempt to substitute pleasure for pain both illustrate and contribute to this pendulum swing. This is because freedom without responsibility makes people prisoners of impulse and restricts their range of activity accordingly.

One way of describing the maturation process from infancy on is to say that it consists of learning to postpone immediate impulse gratification for the sake of more distant goals. In order to accomplish this, not only discipline, but imagination must be trained. The child who wants to be in the school play must have the ability to imagine how pleasurable and satisfying that future event will be, otherwise it will be difficult or impossible to give up afternoons of aimless fun with friends in order to sustain the discipline of rehearsals. With age, the time scale becomes more protracted. Those who wish to prepare for a demanding profession must be able to sustain the discipline of years of education and to sacrifice innumerable occasions of more immediate and transitory pleasures for the sake of the future goal. This effort would be impossible without the ability to retain in the imagination a lively idea of the eventual rewards. At the extreme end of those who have failed to learn this essential lesson stands the addict: the immediate impulse for pleasure or relief of discomfort takes precedence over all other goals. The future is simply unreal to such people and so at the moment of temptation the sustaining power of imagination fails them utterly. Their compulsive seizure of the freedom to do as they please while refusing all responsibility turns their illusory vision of paradise into the bitterest of prisons. Precisely to the extent that people learn to take responsibility for their own situation—with respect both to their interior attitudes and dispositions and their relations with others in the world—do they gain some real freedom, as distinct from the transient gratifications of mere license. Without this kind of responsible freedom, there can be no growth of the personality, no liberation of its creative energies. It is obvious that this process requires the formation of a value system and the practice of constant reference to that system, otherwise there can be no standard for what constitutes responsibility in a given situation, no reference point against which choice between alternatives can be measured. Freud understood these principles very well; that is why, in the course of his lifelong attempt to combat the constricting effects of poor resolutions of unconscious conflict, he insisted on the concept of personal responsibility. He would be the first to be horrified by those modern interpreters, not to say perverters, of his thought who have twisted his creative and subtle insights about the nature and dangers of repression into a false justification for the mindless slogan "If it feels good, do it." Others who have understood Freud's point but do not like it are now attacking his conflict theory directly.

Christianity is under attack for exactly parallel reasons. People have always, and especially recently, objected to the concept of sin, particularly in the form known to theologians as "original sin." This ancient and difficult doctrine is defined in the *New Catholic Encyclopedia* as "hereditary sin incurred at conception by every human being as a result of the original sinful choice of the first man, Adam." This is further qualified as "a condition of guilt, weakness, or debility found in human beings . . . prior to their own freed option for good or evil. A state of being, not an act or its consequences." This is frequently perceived as a cruel and hateful doctrine whereby people are condemned before they even begin life. Assaulted by such a burden of unearned guilt, how could anyone avoid frustration, anger, and all the other negative emotions which are assumed to be the "real" cause underlying deviant behavior?

There is no question that at various times this doctrine has been shamefully abused. A case in point is the belief in infant damnation, which held that the souls of unbaptized babies would perish in a literal hell. In somewhat varying forms this notion was common to Calvinists and Roman Catholics. The doctrine of original sin was also used, from time to time, to justify extremely punitive systems of child-rearing which undoubtedly wreaked spiritual as well as psychological havoc on the unfortunate victims. But there is no idea or system of thought, however nobly or powerfully conceived, which is not subject to human abuse, whether through ignorance or through malice. Those wishing to take exception to the stern excesses of Calvinism, of pre-Vatican II Roman Catholicism, or (even more strongly) to those cynically sinful ecclesiastics--where or whensoever situated throughout Christian history—who have shamefully manipulated the guilt feelings of the poor and the ignorant in the interest of maintaining an economically and politically unjust status quo, are perfectly free to do so. In fact, I number myself among them. We should not, however, allow ourselves to forget that in contemporary abuses of the doctrine of original sin we have not necessarily said anything about the doctrine itself.

The definition I quoted locates the origin of the doctrine in the ancient myth of the Fall. There are those, be they scientists or theologians, who consider the sacred myths to be merely quaint or superstitious remnants of the childhood of the race, surely no help and perhaps even harmful in dealing with the complexities of life in the twentieth century. Such persons would do well to pause and reflect; there may be a certain *hubris* in thus cavalierly discarding this ancient heritage, the only thing which, through all the vicissitudes of varying interpretations, has consistently captured the imagination, commanded the loyalty, and informed the conscience of the majority of folk in the West for two millennia, and (in the case of the Old Testament) has done the same for our religious ancestors, the Jewish people, for much longer than that. There is also a certain lack of logic in continuing to reject the myths on the basis of allegedly superior, enlightened reason in the very century which has seen the discovery of the imaginative power and mysterious energies of the unconscious mind. As the great theologian Reinhold Niebuhr expressed it, the myths are to be taken seriously but not literally. It is in the very nature of sacred myths to speak differently to different people at different times, since they are fundamentally symbolic and archetypal in character, with meaning and power far beyond the limits of any one person's mind, or even beyond the *zeitgeist* of a whole era. It is for this reason that intellectual arguments about which interpretation is "correct" are, in the main, foolish. We are not, after all, dealing with mathematics or with the chemical composition of some unknown substance. Each discipline has its appropriate methodology, and techniques appropriate to the exact sciences are inappropriate here. Both biblical literalists and biblical debunkers have made this error of misplaced precision and concreteness. Space does not permit an adequate description of the methods which are appropriate to the study of the significance of a sacred myth, but it must at least be said that one essential ingredient is an attitude of receptive contemplation, in principle not unlike the approach to a work of art or to the meaning of a dream.

The accounts in Genesis of Adam and Eve in the Garden of Eden contain numerous elements whose richly symbolic character bears on many different aspects of human experience. I excerpt here those parts concerned with the doctrine of original sin.

Yahweh God planted a garden in Eden which is in the east. . . . Yahweh God caused to spring up from the soil every kind of tree, enticing to look at and good to eat, with the tree of life and the tree of the knowledge of good and evil in the middle of the garden. A river flowed from Eden to water the garden. . . . Yahweh God took the man and settled him in the Garden of Eden to cultivate it and take care of it. Then Yahweh God gave this admonition, "You may eat indeed of all of the trees in the garden. Nevertheless of the tree of the knowledge of good and evil you are not to eat, for on the day you eat of it you shall most surely die." . . . The serpent was the most subtle of all the wild beasts that Yahweh God had made. It asked the woman, "Did God really say you were not to eat from any of the trees in the garden?" The woman answered the serpent, "We may eat the fruit of the trees in the garden. But of the fruit of the tree in the middle of the garden God said, "You must not eat it, nor touch it, under pain of death." Then the serpent said to the woman, "No! You will not die! God knows in fact that on the day you eat it your eyes will be opened and you will be like gods, knowing good and evil." The woman saw that the tree was good to eat and pleasing to the eye, and that it was desirable for the knowledge that it could give. So she took some of its fruit and ate it. She gave some also to her husband who was with her, and he ate it. Then the eyes of both of them were opened and they realised that they were naked. So they sewed fig-leaves together to make themselves loin cloths.[1]

In order to appreciate this story in terms which are neither constricted nor superstitious, it is necessary to remember that science and theology must be partners, not adversaries. Any interpretation which is to speak to our modern condition must therefore take into account that biological evolution has been established as a fact. (That there is still dispute in scientific circles about many aspects of this process is not relevant to the level of generality which I am engaging.) If we are not to fall into the dualist heresy, which postulates an unbridgeable split between spirit and matter, we must recognize that biological evolution necessarily implies evolution of consciousness as well. This point of view is central to the following reading of the myth.

It is hard for me to imagine that God would have put the tree in the Garden merely to demonstrate His power and authority; these were already amply manifest. Furthermore, He could hardly have intended the tree as a perpetual temptation. To tempt His creatures thus would have been to commit the same sin for which He cursed the serpent. Why, then, was it there? Doubtless, at some future time when they had learned and experienced enough to be ready for it, God

Himself intended to extend to humankind the knowledge of good and evil. What the serpent wickedly brought about, then, was the premature development of the capacity for choice between good and evil. A modern analogy may illustrate this interpretation. Parents owning an automobile would naturally not permit their young children to drive it, but would expect to teach them when they reached the proper age. A neighbor who, with deceitfully reassuring words, gave a seven-year-old the keys and urged her to take a spin with her brother would be a monster, particularly if, to carry the analogy still further, some dreadful accident ensued and the children were injured to such an extent that their subsequently healthy development was permanently impaired.

What is the symbolic significance of the fact that as soon as Adam and Eve had eaten the fruit they suddenly realized that they were naked? In his book, *Privacy and Freedom,* Alan Westin convincingly demonstrates that the exercise of conscience is always private.[2] People may share with others the fruit of their deliberations about right and wrong, but the essential decisions are solitary. The realization of nakedness is a realization of the need for privacy which would have been unnecessary for Adam and Eve before they had acquired the knowledge of good and evil. Prior to that there would have been no occasion for the solitary exercise of conscience. Why were the sexual organs singled out as in special need of covering? Because these are the organs of intimacy; on the continuum of possible degrees of relationship, the sexual embrace is at the opposite pole to privacy. Contrary to former theological views long since abandoned, but erroneously imagined by many laypeople to be still current, this interpretation of the myth does not equate the sinless state of Adam and Eve before the Fall with sexual innocence. The literal view of Adam and Eve as the actual first human beings is given up. Instead they are understood to be symbolic of our earliest prehistoric ancestors at the dawn of primitive consciousness, naturally subject to all of the usual biological processes. The premature knowledge of good and evil cannot then be thought of as a result of sex. On the other hand, since, as we have seen, sex is one thread in the web of culture, it follows that such knowledge

—and the consequent inevitability of choice by those inadequately equipped to exercise it wisely—would unavoidably affect decisions in the area of sexuality along with all other behavior.

Through all the various interpretations of this myth over the centuries (of which I am sure mine is not the last—nor will it be the last to be considered quaint or even in some sense oppressive) one thread has remained constant. It has always been unmistakably understood to mean that all people, always, everywhere, under all circumstances, at all ages, are responsible for all of their choices, whether these are intentional or accidental. Furthermore, it has been noted that a troublesome number of those choices turn out to be bad ones. The most cursory survey of history, or the daily newspaper, or the behavior of one's friends and relatives, demonstrates the ubiquity of the bad choices made by other people. While far more painful and difficult, a really honest survey of oneself—whether this be undertaken in the confessional, or naked and alone in a white room with one's conscience, or on a psychoanalyst's couch—demonstrates that one is, alas, no exception to this general rule.

It goes without saying that these conditions produce an enormous amount of guilt, both individual and collective. Freud's research revealed the fact that people are subject to guilt for sinful wishes in early childhood that were not even conscious, let alone acted upon, and that these guilt feelings were a major cause of the disposition to psychological disorder in adult life. The point of convergence with more classical religious views becomes evident when we now refer back to the theological description of original sin given earlier: "a condition of guilt, weakness, or debility found in human beings . . . prior to their own free option for good or evil. A state of being, not an act or its consequence." In describing the infantile and childhood processes of choice in the resolution of conflict, Freud has surely exposed a significant part of the anatomy and physiology, so to speak, of what we have been referring to for centuries as original sin.

The concept of responsibility is central both to the psychoanalytic and the religious view of the human condition. In the religious view, it is grounded in the myth; our archaic parents Adam and Eve and, by virtue of our kinship with them, we also are individually responsible to God. That mysterious Word is the traditional Name given to the essential Archimedean reference point outside the self without which no man or woman would have the essential leverage to rise beyond the constricting unfreedoms of irrational impulse, and would instead remain in the imprisoning collectivity of massmindedness. As we have seen, no freedom is possible without a firmly anchored sense of responsibility. It is this liberating insight which is captured in the words of the Episcopal Book of Common Prayer: "O God, who art the author of peace and lover of concord, in knowledge of whom standeth our eternal life, *whose service is perfect freedom.* . . ."[3]

Freud, on the other hand, addressed himself primarily to the explanation of guilt itself, and invented a myth of his own—that of the prehistoric parricide—to account for it. In addition to being subject to the logical objection that it presupposes the very thing it is trying to explain, this man-made myth has also proved vulnerable to the sophisticated research of modern anthropology. But these objections to the inadequacy of Freud's speculations about the origin of guilt must not blind us to the magnitude of his contribution to our understanding of its subtle, invisible mechanics in the depths of the human psyche. These include the fact that its burdens are cumulative if it remains undealt with, and may cause a destructive proliferation both of attitudes which inhibit further growth, and behavior which provokes further guilt. Much of what Freud studied, of course, we would unhesitatingly label neurotic guilt. By this we mean either that the original sinful deed or wish is largely fanciful, or that the quantity of guilt experienced is out of all proportion to the extent of its cause. This kind of guilt did not, of course, entirely escape the notice of theologians and one form of it has for centuries been known in a rudimentary way as "scrupulosity." (In the light of our new knowledge, this would now be called obsessive-compulsiveness.) What was not known, however, was that an excessive emphasis on the concept of sin, particularly when this was at the expense of appropriate emphasis on the equally important joyful doctrines, could seriously aggravate guilt of all kinds.

The major religions of the West have always had ways, and very effective ones when properly understood and practiced, of dealing with guilt. In addition to regular observances throughout the year, the Jewish religion has the great annual High Holy Days—Rosh Hashana, the New Year, through Yom Kippur, the Day of Atonement. In the Christian religion, atonement is linked to the death and resurrection of Christ. This is reified in the believer's experience in several ways, the most dramatic of which is known in various denominations as the Holy Communion, Holy Eucharist, the Mass, or the Divine Liturgy. The public, corporate confession of sin and absolution of guilt is an integral part of this ritual. The atonement process is further underlined in most branches of Christianity by the annual observance of Lent and Holy Week.

In Chapter One we examined some of the reasons for the decline of religion as the dominant cohesive element in Western culture. (This may yet be the salvation of religion, since it is now removed from the temptations of politics and temporal power which contributed so heavily to its abuses over the centuries. One may even speculate that the astonishing strength and relative purity of the Jewish tradition may have been facilitated by the fact that its minority position prevented it from being subject to these corrupting temptations.) In Chapter Nine we went on to see that the wholesale substitution of the concept of sickness for the concept of sin has not changed the characteristically uncharitable ways people treat each other. There was great initial hope in many quarters that if people could be delivered from the superstitious bondage of their guilt-provoking religions, and if systems of child-rearing informed by the insights of the new science of psychoanalysis could be widely implemented, the world would become a much better place. Alas, this Freudian millennium has failed to materialize. There is not only no noticeable improvement in the level of public morality, but things are, if anything, worse. Karl Menninger, that grand old man of American psychoanalysis has written a most thought-provoking book, the kernel of whose message is contained in the title: *What Ever Became of Sin?*[4]

The doctrine of original sin should have been used to point to the perfect, to prevent pride by emphasizing that it is impossible not to sin, to underscore the concept of personal responsibility, and to encourage growth by showing that there will always be some inner problem left to challenge us. The concept of illness in the psychological and emotional fields should have been used to illuminate the concept of sin, not to replace it. It should have been used to assist us in understanding the dynamics of particular failures, to illuminate the virtue of mercy, to bring wisdom to the delicate processes involved both in penitence and in absolution. But just as the concept of sin was often abused by those who, lost in personal power and pride, wished to dominate and control others while hiding behind a cynical pretense of saving their souls, so the concept of illness is now being abused in parallel ways, and for the same sinful reasons. It is therefore not surprising that some people, including many so-called experts, are now trying to reject both, leaving our civilization teetering on the brink of social disaster which is both sinful *and* sick.

As we look around us, it becomes clear that the real issue is not guilt, but responsibility. For every person who suffers from guilt which is out of all proportion to any offenses they may have committed, there is another whose quantum of guilt is totally inadequate to the magnitude of their misdeeds. In each case the balance between freedom and responsibility is seriously disturbed. Psychotherapists tend to see those people whose unconscious burden of neurotic guilt is excessive; this inhibits their freedom to mature and often leads to behavior which, from the standpoint of society, is irresponsible. On the other hand, the Nuremberg trials of Nazi war criminals and the trial of Adolf Eichmann were the attempt of an outraged civilization to deal with people whose sense of guilt was totally inadequate.

What troubled people need, through the appropriate application of religious and psychiatric categories, either singly or in combination, is to learn to take serious responsibility for their attitudes, behavior and circumstances. Included in this process must be not only those issues which are contemporary and conscious. As the twig is bent, so grows the tree. Wrong choices made in the past prevent healthy development and therefore contribute to present problems.

Viewed in these terms, every failure to take a possible maturational step has moral significance and falls under the rubric of original sin, that doctrine which accounts for the fact that human beings are simply incapable of always choosing wisely and require constant help, love, and guidance to learn to do better. We have also seen that this is true even if the person's responsibility is mitigated by the process having taken place unconsciously. It is impossible for homosexuality not to be included in this category. By the same token, *all* failures of maturation are to be viewed similarly, and there is no reason to single out homosexuality for cruel and unusual condemnation. Every un-wanted pregnancy, every divorce, all spouses driven to rage, infidelity, alcoholism, or drugs by the insensitivity and rejection of their partner —all these are to be included as well. But our culture's attempts to bring humane understanding to these situations and to preserve the decency and dignity of those caught in them is often misguided. For instance, there is a growing trend to revise the laws in favor of some-thing called "no-fault divorce." This is wrong, as it encourages the current tendency to abdication of responsibility. The proper term would be "shared-fault divorce."

Homosexuality then cannot be viewed as a perfectly normal alter-nate lifestyle. As we have seen earlier, it comes in many varieties, not all of which are accompanied by other obvious failures of personality development or adjustment, or by other unacceptable or socially un-desirable behavior. If one speaks of homosexual acts taking place between two consenting adults in private in the context of an ongoing relationship between the partners, even though the homosexual dispo-sition itself constitutes an immaturity, it surely ranks well below many other immaturities in the amount of social or moral harm which is done. For instance, the unresolved sibling rivalry which in adult life is acted out in the form of malicious gossip about others is far worse, far more obviously sinful.

It seems to me that the Church is involved in a gradual, important, and long overdue change. Instead of dealing with sexual aberrations almost exclusively through the harsh processes of judgment and con-demnation, it is learning to deal with them in the penitential mode, through compassion and forgiveness extended to those who are doing their best to take responsibility for their lives. With respect to such things as divorce and illegitimacy, the change is nearly complete. With respect to adultery and abortion, it is well underway. With respect to homosexuality, it is just beginning. I believe that homosexuals who try to claim that their condition is normal are in danger of impeding this necessary change.

Far from proclaiming their condition to be normal, homosexuals have the responsibility to minimize it as far as this lies within their power. For some, this may entail the long process of change to the heterosexual adaptation, with or without the assistance of therapy. For others, the decision may be to choose a celibate lifestyle. That, however, is not possible for everyone without crippling them in other ways, and it is unreasonable and cruel to demand it. Those who cannot change or abstain must make the attempt to express their sexual nature in the most stable, responsible, and loving forms of which they are capable. Only in this way is it possible to avoid adding sins to sin, a responsibility which is incumbent on every one of us, certainly not only or in any special way on homosexuals.

It must be emphasized, however, that the growing opinion that homosexuality is perfectly normal and does not constitute immaturity (or any other term by which we may designate evidences of original sin) is positively harmful; it is most important that it be categorically rejected. In addition to theological considerations about the spread of sin, these views should be rejected because of the effect of such a climate of opinion on the young. As we have seen, adolescence is a period which requires the utmost of young people in working their way through the enormously difficult transition from childhood to adulthood. In particular, it involves a period of sexual uncertainty and experimentation. The tendency toward adolescent experimentation is in general a good one, since it encourages the development of independence and is essential to the trial and error method by which most people finally arrive at their choice of life work. To a certain extent it is valuable sexually—one should get to know many people of the opposite sex before finally choosing what one hopes will be a mate for life. At the same time, the anxieties surrounding the psychosexual maturation process are severe, and the temptation to opt for less than one is capable of is very great. While it is probably true that one cannot proselytize the invulnerable, there are a great many youngsters whose childhoods have been sufficiently problematic so that homosexuality presented to them as an acceptable alternative would be convincingly attractive.

In some states where the criminal laws against homosexuality have been repealed, activist organizations are already beginning to demand (using the American Psychiatric Association nomenclature change discussed in Chapter Four as support) that sex education courses in schools include the presentation of the homosexual lifestyle as an alternative. This is a perfectly logical and inevitable consequence of the premise that homosexuality is in no way abnormal. While I favor the repeal of the criminal statutes, this repeal must not happen on the basis that homosexuality is normal, but on the entirely different legal principle that sexual acts taking place in private between consenting adults should be beyond the reach of the law. Nor is this dangerous trend confined to the secular arm of the homosexual culture. The following quotation is taken from a recent book by one of the founders of Dignity, an organization of homosexual Roman Catholic priests:

> Another function which the Christian homosexual community can perform is that of providing models. Homosexuals, especially the young, have a desperate need of models of what it means to live out a full human life as a homosexual.[5]

He goes on to suggest that Dignity should concern itself with providing the equivalent of premarital counseling to young homosexual couples. While I respect the author's sincerity and good intentions, I utterly reject what he says. It is impossible for me to state strongly enough that to present this model to young people, or to allow them —as often happens in the contemporary climate of open discussion— to imagine that their transitory adolescent experiments are truly indicative of a settled homosexual disposition, is not only evidence of psychiatric ignorance, but is specifically wicked as well.

In spite of these strong statements, I cannot conclude this chapter without saying that the immaturity which homosexuality represents, even though it is morally significant, cannot possibly be as distasteful to the sight of God as the self-righteous hostility of those who persecute homosexuals. Nor is there any room for the milder attitudes of patronizing condescension to "unfortunates." The first law of God, and also the last, is real charity to all. It is incumbent on *all* of us to keep it.

12
The Goals of Human Sexuality Reconsidered

The recent book, *The Church and the Homosexual,* by John J. McNeill, a Jesuit priest and moral theologian, provides an excellent demonstration of my contention that one's view of the goals of human sexuality is absolutely fundamental to any decision about the morality of homosexuality. (This consideration applies with equal force to the assessment of particular modes of heterosexual behavior.) Before taking issue with Father McNeill's position, however, I should like to commend him in one important respect. He understands very well that we are in the process of a serious revision of our traditional attitudes toward sexuality and that this task must be addressed both scientifically and theologically. He knows that sexual behavior does have moral significance which, as we have seen, many polemicists are now trying to deny. While neither he nor I would wish to see a return to the legalistic and guilt-ridden rigidity of the sexual codes of the past, we can agree that there is a very real difference between the *evolution* of sexual morality and the *dissolution* which threatens us in the West today. At this point, however, Father McNeill and I part company.

His first thesis is that "the homosexual condition is according to the will of God. God so created humans that their sexuality is not determined by their biology."[1] His arguments here rest on the common misinterpretations of psychological and anthropological evidence which I reviewed and discussed in Part II: while it is true that sexuality is not reducible to its biological aspects, it is inarguable that the heterosexual disposition is that which biology dictates, and unless there is an inhibiting disturbance in the acculturation process, people do not become fixed in an adult homosexual adaptation.

He also believes that, to the extent that the homosexual disposition is a result of unconscious conditioning in childhood, it is morally neutral, since it comes about "through no fault of their own."[2] Earlier, I argued that unconscious solutions to conflict *are* the result of choice and that people *are* responsible for such choices. I interpreted the sacred myth of the Fall of Adam and Eve in terms of the premature development of the capacity for choice between good and evil. This unmanageable burden is expressed in the developing psyche of each human being precisely in the empirically demonstrable fact that we *do* choose unconsciously between alternatives; furthermore, because this process begins so early in life that we have neither the necessary experience or judgment to choose wisely, all of us are, to a greater or lesser degree, deformed by our past. As adults, we are constituted by all that has happened to us and by all of our responses to the sum of those internal and external events. In theological language, we are all miserable sinners. Precisely the same phenomenon is being described in psychiatric language by those who point out that *everybody,* if you really take a thorough look at the depths of their psyche, is at least a little bit neurotic.

McNeill's argument that the homosexual condition is divinely willed further rests on his belief that "always and everywhere a certain percentage of humans"[3] are subject to the condition. I find this view astonishing and dangerous. While the section of his book in which this argument is developed is well informed by much responsible scholarship, *at bottom* it rests on the circular fallacy in which statistics are cited as the basis for value judgments, but those judgments are actually antecedent to the examination of the data. I am certain that if Father McNeill had been considering the fact that "always and everywhere" a certain percentage of people are habitually inclined to acts of violence, he would have applied his learning and his faculty for subtle argument in a completely different way. We would not hear that violence "is according to the will of God."

Parenthetically, it should be noted that homosexuality does *not* occur "always and everywhere." A striking exception is the People's Republic of China. Lynn Turgeon, reporting on a visit to that country writes:

> When one of our group asked about homosexuality, none of the young Chinese [medical staff] at the Canton Hospital seemed to know what the questioner was talking about. Finally, a seventy-three-year-old doctor, the hospital's chief of staff, had to explain what was meant by the question.[4]

On first reading this report I was so astonished that I took the trouble to verify it by questioning several of my medical colleagues who have been to China. They confirmed it. It appears to be the result of Chairman Mao's decision to place the sexual thread in the web of Chinese culture very differently from its disposition in the fabric of Western society. Several reports have been published by American doctors returning from visits to China, and they all agree that venereal disease has been completely wiped out in that country. There is also no illegitimacy and no extramarital intercourse, in spite of the fact that late marriage (in the middle twenties) is the rule. Birth control is widely practiced and families are limited to two, or at most three, children. From the available evidence, I conclude that the disappearance of homosexuality is the result of two factors: the child-rearing practices and the role of women.

Lynn Turgeon describes a visit to a crèche run by a factory for the workers' children:

> Here, children from less than one year to about the age of six are cared for. There are two hundred and fifty children in all. For the youngest, a group of about twenty infants, three women are specifically assigned. The children are taken home only on weekends, Saturday night to Monday morning. Children prefer living in to going home nightly, which is possible.[5]

Such a system, exposing children from infancy to the care and supervision of adults other than their parents and significantly reducing the amount of time spent in the family household, does not permit the atmosphere of intense, exclusive intimacy prevailing in Western families, where all of the unconscious processes of the child's psychosexual development are focused mainly on relationships with the parents. The system therefore affords excellent protection against the development of the kinds of family patterns from which homosexuality emerges. (This interpretation is further supported by the fact that homosexuality is virtually unknown in those persons who have been raised in Israeli kibbutzim.) Furthermore, the Chinese system does not, in contrast to Western ways, encourage the development of *individual* competitiveness and aggressiveness, either for males or females. These qualities are fostered in group or team settings only. We saw earlier that disturbances in the development and expression of these traits contribute heavily to the homosexual disposition, especially in males.

The role of women in China is also extremely different from their role in the West. No Chinese woman is socialized into believing that motherhood is her primary or highest calling. Everyone is expected to work outside the home, women as well as men, and all are trained for a job or profession. Women are not excluded from any endeavor on the basis of sex alone. Clothing for men and women is, to Western eyes, similar, and in no way sexually provocative. It is not considered appropriate to make even the mildest of sexual overtures to any woman with whom a friendship has not first been cultivated. When I was in Leningrad in 1969 I met a Dutch traveling salesman who had been to China on business. He reported that on one occasion an associate of his, who had not been to China previously and was therefore unfamiliar with the customs, whistled at a pretty girl in the street. He was immediately apprehended and taken to the police station. There it was carefully and lengthily explained to him that such behavior was insulting to the dignity of women and that therefore no Chinese man would ever do such a thing. The spirit of this explanation was patronizing, as to a poor benighted foreigner who couldn't really be expected to know better—not unlike the spirit in which our own nineteenth-century missionaries explained to natives that they really ought to wear clothes. The general prevalence of the sexual attitude to women illustrated by this anecdote has been confirmed by other travelers I have questioned since. We have already seen that a mother's damaged sense of her own competence and mature femininity is an important factor in the development of homosexuality in her children. We have also seen that far too many women in our culture are still urged to limit their view of femininity to sexual allure. It is clear that the social conditions reported from China would go far to alleviate this kind of maternal contribution to the homosexual problem.

To some readers, this description of the sexual customs in China may sound like a foretaste of the millennium; to others it may seem more like a page out of *1984*, George Orwell's prophecy of doom. Without commenting on the price paid by the Chinese people to achieve a change of such magnitude in a mere thirty years, a price which might well be wholly unacceptable to Western political and libertarian sensibilities, let me emphasize two points which the Chinese phenomenon proves beyond a reasonable doubt. First, homosexuality, far from being an innate disposition which will inevitably assert itself in some proportion of any population, is definitely the result of patterns of child-rearing and acculturation. Secondly, since the eradication of homosexuality was not the primary aim of the Chinese leaders and its disappearance was essentially a side effect of the effort to implement other, larger goals (such as the eradication of veneral disease and the social problem of illegitimacy), homosexuality cannot be considered as an independent variable. Its incidence and the shapes of its manifestation are inevitably connected to the general cultural values and attitudes toward sexuality, including the role expectations for both men and women.

It would be interesting to know in just what terms Chairman Mao conceptualized the goals of human sexuality—if indeed he ever addressed the question in that form at all. One thing is certain: he retained a lively appreciation of the distinction between lust and desire for the beloved, perhaps drawing on the ancient Chinese wisdom of the *I Ching,* which teaches that "it is perseverance that makes the difference between seduction and courtship."[6]

Father McNeill has made his own views about the goals of sexuality clear in the following passage taken from the epilogue of his book:

> I hope in the near future to explore a new ethical understanding of human sexuality as a form of human play—where play is understood as any action which has its meaning in itself in the here-and-now; that is to say, an action that is end-in-itself, just as the person is end-in-himself or herself.[7]

My objections to this statement are manifold. In the first place, I find the notion that a person is "end-in-himself or herself" at least misleading, if not actually false. Earlier in his book this concept of personhood is used in support of attitudes to oneself and to others which forbid exploitation, sexual or otherwise, and which encourage healthy independence and the development of each individual's creative potential. These are worthy aims, but they can be much better and more reliably served by a different concept of personhood, one which accords equal value to community as to individuality. It is well expressed in this quotation from Jung:

> Although the conscious achievement of individuality is consistent with man's natural destiny, it is nevertheless not his whole aim. It cannot possibly be the object of human education to create an anarchic conglomeration of individual existences. That would be too much like the unavowed ideal of extreme individualism, which is essentially no more than a morbid reaction against an equally futile collectivism. In contrast to all this, the natural process of individuation brings to birth a consciousness of human community precisely because it makes us aware of the unconscious, which unites and is common to all mankind. . . . Once the individual is thus secured in himself, there is some guarantee that the organized accumulation of individuals . . . will result in the formation no longer of an anonymous mass but of a conscious community. The indispensable condition for this is conscious freedom of choice and individual decision. Without this freedom and self-determination there is no true community, and, it must

Community (Jung)

be said, without such community even the free and self-secured individual cannot in the long run prosper.[8]

This is a very different picture from that of a person as end-in-himself or herself.

Underlying this difference, which at first sight may appear to be only a shift in emphasis, is a very complex and profound issue which has occupied the Church for centuries. This has to do with the nature of order and of what means are available to human beings for discerning it; theologians refer to the principle in question as "natural law." Father McNeill is aware that this is central to the discussion and repudiates it in the following words:

> I believe the most radical difference in the approach to a moral evaluation of homosexuality between Charles Curran [a Roman Catholic theologian] and myself is that, as I understand it, he is still working within a natural law context which allows him to make such theoretical distinctions as "objective" versus "subjective" sin. Whereas in contrast *I am approaching the problem from a personalist philosophical perspective* where such a distinction would be meaningless.[9]

Greek philosophers were deeply concerned with the question of natural law. In the thirteenth century St. Thomas Aquinas developed the principle extensively along Christian lines, equating it with divine law as it is accessible to human reason. Because the dynamic and evolutionary character of the universe, including all of its sentient creatures, was not appreciated, such considerations were not included in the manifold elaborations and applications of the principle, particularly in the field of moral theology. In addition, it stressed reason at the expense of observation. These defects rendered natural law theory vulnerable to serious criticism from the developing empirical sciences. It continued, however, to form the basis for many of the developments in legal and political theory during this same period. There has been a considerable revival of it in the twentieth century, and this is evident in such things as the United Nations Charter and the legal principles used in the Nuremberg trials, which depend on concepts of inalienable human rights and natural freedoms. *The New Catholic Encyclopedia* defines it as "a law or rule of action that is implicit in the very nature of things . . . the imprint of God's providential plan on man's natural reason." Such an idea is clearly the very antithesis of a personalist philosophy which conceives of individuals as ends in themselves.

Some concept of natural law, in one form or another, is extremely widespread, if not universal, in human history and culture. The ancient Chinese wisdom contained in the *I Ching* is an important example. The book is divided into sixty-four sections, each of which has six variations. These are all depicted in symbolic patterns of lines, with accompanying text expressed in short, poetic images, mainly drawn from the world of nature. The text is designed to be used as an oracle, by means of a special ceremony of reverent consultation. In China, for at least 2,000 years, it was believed that all possible human situations or predicaments could be clarified by the understandings this book made possible, all of which depend on relating the specific instance to a more general pattern preexisting in nature, which was divinely constituted and given and from which it was perilous to depart.

Somewhat closer to our own tradition, and exercising considerable influence on a number of medieval Christian mystics, is the Jewish system preserved to this day in Hassidic mysticism. Here the divinely given pattern is the Tree of Life, which is divided into Ten Holy Sephiroth, or spheres. These are connected by twenty-two paths, one for each letter of the Hebrew alphabet. All possible objects, events, or situations, whether on the cosmic or human planes, are considered to have a reference point in the pattern of the Tree. The spheres relate to the essential or static aspects of things, while the paths between the spheres illuminate the dynamic connections. Systems of religious divination were devised also, in order to consult the Wisdom of the Tree in times of stress or doubt.

It is to all such theories of natural law that J. M. Cameron is appealing in the passage I quoted at the end of Chapter Ten: "There is no feeling for the immensely old human tradition of venerating the powers of sexuality . . . an attitude for which the sexual is . . . a part of the *sacred order of the cosmos.* "[10] In a secular and partial form, of course, this principle is the one which is reasserting itself as the basis for the ecology movement. We are perforce discovering that the "sacred order" cannot be wantonly disturbed, that we do not stand outside of it in some position of control and command, but must submit to it far more deeply than our proud, empirical rationality would have liked. God is not mocked with impunity.

William Temple, the late Archbishop of Canterbury, applied this idea of sacred order to the field of human relations in a way which includes, but is by no means limited to, the aforementioned concepts of inalienable human rights and the wise use of natural resources. He had a vision of the sacramental universe in which moral progress is defined as widening one's circle of allegiance. In applying the divine law, "Love thy neighbor," eventually all persons, no matter how distant, are to be vividly experienced as "neighbors."

The problems, of course, arise in attempting to apply the notion of natural law, as it was developed in the Christian tradition, to particular human situations, especially when these involve some ethical or moral dilemma. In fact, much that has been written in this area, particularly by pre-Vatican II Roman Catholic theologians, is completely foreign to any modern thought patterns, except possibly to those of a relentlessly ecclesiastical turn of mind. This is because primary reliance is placed on reason as the chief instrument of discerning the manifestations of natural law. The faculties of sense perception, intuition, and feeling are either ignored, or considered to have minimal contributions to make to the issue, or perceived as actual hindrances to be subdued in the course of the effort to arrive at the truth.

The research of modern depth psychology has exposed the self-defeating quality of this excessively rational approach. Freud's original discoveries about the energy and ambiguity of the unconscious dethroned reason and will from their previously supposed sovereignty over the mind. But the idea of reason enthroned dies hard, and in the Freudian system there is a certain tendency to view the unconscious as a sort of mental sewer which contains all of the primitive, instinctual, archaic and perverse—all that makes trouble within and between people. Freud's idea of maturation, and of the process of ridding oneself of neurotic tendencies, is expressed in his own aphorism: "Where *id* was, let *ego* be." While the ego is not equated with rationality itself, its function is nevertheless importantly characterized by the process of applying one's reason to the ordering and management of unconscious contents as these gradually emerge.

However, as we have seen, Freud still believed that people were ultimately morally responsible, even though frequently helpless, for decisions made unconsciously. Theologians, in the course of their praiseworthy attempts to familiarize themselves with the new scientific discoveries about human psychology, have frequently misunderstood the unconscious. In the old days they knew better than to accept the common excuse "It's not my fault, the Devil tempted me!" Too often they have uncritically accepted "I couldn't help it, my unconscious betrayed me," without realizing that the two statements are morally identical, both involving rejection of personal responsibility. To use the concept of the unconscious in this way is to do both psychology and religion a great disservice.

Jung's view of the psyche is considerably more sophisticated and inclusive. Far from perceiving the unconscious mainly as a storehouse of the irrational, troublesome or undesirable (although he realized that it did indeed contain such elements), he recognized it as the human receptor organ for divine revelation. Not only the worst, but the best emerges through unconscious depths. Instead of a simple distinction between the rational (good, safe, reliable) and the irrational (bad, dangerous, unpredictable), he described four psychological functions of equal importance, each of which can manifest itself either consciously or unconsciously. Some are rational and some *nonrational;* but none is intrinsically *irrational.* These are *feeling, intuition, thinking,* and *sensing.* Feeling refers to that mode of judging which assigns emotional or moral value to things and is thus distinct from the thinking function, which evaluates things according to whether they are logically true or false. Sensing refers to the ability to relate in a concrete and practical way to outer reality.

I have been struck by the correspondence of these functions to those mentioned in the summary of the Law: "Thou shalt love the Lord thy God with all thy *heart, soul, mind* and *strength.*" Clearly the over-valuation of reason at the expense of the other faculties is not something enjoined on us by God, but a distortion we have invented for ourselves and which is particularly rampant in Western culture. It has seriously contaminated the discipline of theology; this in part accounts for the rise in popularity (at all levels, from the groves of Academe to the street) of Eastern religions, mystical sects, and the charismatic movement. These all speak to one or more of the relatively neglected faculties of feeling, intuition and sensing. While it is true that much contemporary Christian practice pays lip service to these needs, it is all too customary to address them indirectly, through the mind. Such efforts quickly tend to deteriorate into a "head trip." By contrast, the Eastern, mystical and charismatic approaches engage these faculties directly, in their own terms, and, at their best, they also draw on the largely untapped resources inherent in the confident exercise of these functions. We return here to another meaning of Rosemary Haughton's statement that "theology cannot be done in an intellectual laboratory."[11]

Besides this overemphasis on reason, there is another error which besets those attempting to apply the concept of the natural law to the moral understanding of particular human dilemmas. This is the failure to distinguish accurately between principles and rules. Principles do not change. Rules are the cultural clothes worn by a principle; they are suited to the needs of a particular time, place and situation. For example, we now perceive that St. Paul's cultural context has been outgrown and we therefore feel free to reject his specific *rules* for the conduct of women; nevertheless, we still must subscribe to his timeless *principle* that in the house of God "everything must be done with propriety and in order" (I Corinthians 14:40). St. Paul's own distinction between the spirit and the letter of the law illustrates this point —spirit corresponding to what I have called principles, and letter corresponding to rules.[12] But without the assumption not only of existence, but of the immutability of natural law, it becomes extraordinarily difficult to lay hold of principles in any firm way; consequently one's evaluation of rules becomes dangerously pragmatic. The essential reference point outside the self becomes too distant and too abstract to be reliably useful as an anchor for the responsible exercise of conscience.

In the effort to avoid this problem, I find the substitution of the phrase "sacred order of the cosmos" for the phrase "natural law" extremely useful. The connotations surrounding the word *law* too easily suggest that there are areas of concern or endeavor which are irrelevant to it; so long as the law is not broken, it does not matter one way or the other what one does. Sacred order, on the other hand, lends itself more easily to the inclusion of our new knowledge of the totally dynamic, interdependent and evolutionary character of the universe, and of all of the human faculties on their own terms. We know from modern physics that there is no such thing as complete objectivity, since the observer's mere presence affects that which is being observed, however slightly. Everything really is dependent upon everything else, nothing exists or takes place in isolation from anything else. Nothing is disconnected. Everything matters.

The practical example illustrating this view is the one mentioned earlier, our new appreciation of the principles of ecology. Central to this is a recognition that the human species is not outside of the natural set of relations existing between the animal, mineral and vegetable kingdoms, but is an integral part of it. We are perforce discovering that attempts to dominate our environment lead not only to the murder of Mother Earth, but to our own suicide. What we must learn to do instead is to find our proper place in the pattern, in the sacred order. Within that place will be found our appropriate evolutionary mode and direction. The freedom to grow is contingent upon our taking the responsibility of accepting these limitations.

We see that the sacred order can be best understood, not as a set of laws or rules (although these do exist), but as pattern, as what John Dixon has called the ordering of relation. Essential to this is the rejection of dualism. The body and the psyche are a seamless unity, not separate entities incongruously and awkwardly forced to occupy the same space at the same time during a life span. In an empirical way, the principles and practice of psychosomatic medicine exemplify this complete congruity. On another scale, physicists in this century have discovered that matter and energy are not discontinuous, but are merely different forms of one another, and that the laws governing their behavior are best expressed as a pattern (field theory) describing a set of dynamic relations. Because of the limitations of our sensory-intellectual apparatus, we choose different vocabularies to talk about this principle as it manifests itself on different planes or in different scales. Nevertheless, we can understand the body/mind problem as a special case of the matter/energy problem, and can thus recognize that the pattern of relations is always fundamental and therefore antecedent to the particular form or state in which we may perceive something. The pattern of six-sidedness *precedes* the condensation of moisture into snowflakes, even though no two snowflakes are precisely alike. Somewhat more complexly, if a person is in a disordered pattern of angry relations with others, we may perceive this as a manifestation of the psyche in the form of a display of temper, or we may perceive it as a manifestation of the body in the form of elevated blood pressure. Basic and antecedent to either manifestation is a disordered pattern of relationship.

Even though no two human beings are precisely alike, there is nevertheless a general pattern to which we must conform. As we have seen, this pattern inevitably includes private as well as public behavior. In fact, that very distinction is misleading, since the thoughts we think and the things we do when we are alone are inexorably constitutive of what we are, and unavoidably influence the way we behave in community. Disorder in the pattern of Hitler's private thoughts killed six million Jews. The private thoughts which a man may have about sexuality will influence not only what he does behind the closed doors of his bedroom, but the way in which he looks at women on the street, how he treats his daughters, his business practices toward his female employees—in short, every single relationship he ever has with women, no matter how apparently casual or remote; all this, furthermore, will be true even when there is no question of any departure from the law or custom of his community. Thus we see that the adherence to, or departure from, the pattern takes place at a level which long precedes the level at which laws and rules operate.

I have emphasized three points, all of which require that we give up some of our excessive and unfounded pride in our rationality. First, as a species we do not stand outside the sacred order in some position of control or command, but are a part of it and are subject to its principles and dynamisms. Second, to find, keep and enjoy our right place in this pattern, we must exercise all of our faculties, not merely our reason and will. Last, it is in our totality that we are part of the pattern, body as well as spirit.

Such a view of sacred order completely denies the possibility of the person as "end-in-himself or herself." Nor can there be any activity, play or otherwise, which is an "end-in-itself." To claim otherwise is to set apart areas of endeavor which are somehow outside the pattern. This, I believe, is precisely the nature of sin. Whether unconsciously (original sin), unintentionally through ignorance or lack of serious-ness, or intentionally through the lust of self-centered pride, we distort the pattern of the sacred order. But the powerful dynamisms which animate and direct that order are not so easily transgressed; sooner or later the order proves stronger than our attempts to tamper with it. We are discovering the hard way that the worship of money, power, and materialistic "progress" which led us to despoil the earth brings inexorable punishment. The ancient prohibition against idolatry does not refer only to statues. An idol is anything at all, whether material or spiritual, which is valued for its own sake, as an end-in-itself. Only God is a proper end-in-Himself. We are to enjoy and to do all manner of things, but these must be evaluated and chosen not in their own terms, but according to their ability to point to God and to confirm and support us in our proper place in the sacred order.

The application of these principles to sexuality during Christian history has been seriously contaminated by the major heresy of dual-ism. In the first few centuries, the Church Fathers were greatly con-cerned with combating the various forms of the Gnostic heresy. Gnos-tics held that matter was an evil illusion, that only spirit could partake of the nature of God and the sacred order. It was for this reason that so much stress was laid on the doctrine of the Incarnation, which teaches that Jesus was fully human as well as fully divine. For the same reason, equal emphasis was placed on the bodily resurrection not only of Jesus, but of human beings at the Last Day. The important thrust of both of these doctrines is to counteract the dualism, to insist that both body and psyche are part of the sacred order, that holiness can be found in both.[13]

Unfortunately, remnants of this dualist heresy clung to the skirts of the Church, and manifested itself, for example, in the excesses of ascetical practice designed to subdue the evils of the flesh. In particular, at various times and to varying degrees, this dualism has invaded the teachings of the Church in regard to sex. Until recently, what has filtered down to the general church-going public in most branches of Christianity, especially since the Reformation, has too often been the idea that all sex is bad, homosexuality is even worse, and only marriage with sex for the purpose of procreation redeems any of it; furthermore, how awkward of God not to have thought of a better way to perpetuate the race! Now of course this is a vastly distorted and oversimplified version of what the Church has actually taught, but it has come through in just that form through individual priests and ministers often enough to cause an enormous amount of harm. The whole area of sexual morality has been overlaid with a very heavy burden of hypocrisy and guilt. Such views were bound to be overturned sooner or later because they violate the sacred order in which body and psyche are a seamless unity.

As I have indicated throughout this book, the findings of science have been invaluably helpful in dispelling many of the hindrances of ignorance which encumbered the discipline of theology. But there is a problem here, too. Although the pioneers on the frontiers of science, especially in physics, are now fully aware that the old watertight compartments of space and time, spirit and matter, do not describe the actual state of things, and have thus rendered any belief in the various formulations of the dualist position evidence of mere ignorance, these insights have not yet penetrated the general public consciousness. In the heyday of nineteenth-century deterministic materialism, it was believed that sufficient energetic application of the scientific method would eventually reveal that everything is ultimately reducible to its physical components, even religious experience. This is, of course, the Gnostic heresy in modern dress. The Gnostics held that matter was an evil illusion, whereas science began to hold, and in many quarters still does, that spirit is a foolish illusion.

If in some areas of research scientists happen to entertain this fallacy, no great harm is done. For example, those who investigate the effects of pituitary hormones on rates of bone growth may believe what they like about the materialist hypothesis without affecting the results of their study in any noticeable way. This is, however, emphatically untrue when it comes to the study of sexuality. We saw in earlier chapters that Kinsey and his associates, as well as Masters and Johnson, all made the error of believing that sex could usefully, and without serious distortion, be reduced to its physical aspects. Of all the criticisms which have been leveled against various aspects of Freud's theory, the most serious, and the one with which I fully agree, is that of just this kind of reductionism. His own scientific training was greatly influenced by the mid-nineteenth-century materialism; this was undoubtedly an important influence on his belief that every manifestation of the human psyche was to be explained in terms of its primitive instinctual components. These, he believed, would eventually yield the secrets of their intrinsically chemical nature to further scientific research. He believed in order, but not sacred order, because his thought was fatally contaminated by this dualism.

There is therefore nothing in classical Freudian theory which throws any light on the goals of human sexuality beyond the ultimately physical issues of pleasure and reproduction. Jungian theory offers a very different perspective. The following quotation puts the difference succinctly:

> Freud undoubtedly attributed supreme value to the orgastic release of sex, whereas Jung found supreme value in the unifying experience of religion. Hence Freud tended to interpret all numinous and emotionally significant experience as derived from, or a substitute for, sex; whereas Jung tended

to interpret even sexuality itself as symbolic, possessing "numinous" significance in that it represented an irrational union of opposites and was thus a symbol of wholeness.[14]

For all of his extensive and brilliant research which demonstrated conclusively that most human thought and behavior is symbolic rather than merely literal, Freud failed to understand the true significance of this discovery. He interpreted the symbols only reductionistically, seeing them all as pointing back to some earlier contents of the human psyche. While it is true that in particular neurotic disturbances such interpretations are significantly true and useful, this fact is far from encompassing the full scope and purpose of the human symbolic faculty. Freud failed to see for himself, and went on to refuse to acknowledge it when it was pointed out to him by Jung, that the most important significance of the human symbolic faculty is religious. Images and symbols of the sacred order are intrinsic to the human psyche. Collective representations of them constitute the symbol systems of the religions, and variations on these are to be found in the unconsciously elaborated symbols of individuals. Such images point, not backwards into our own psyche, but to that timeless and spaceless realm of eternity, where there is no here or there, no before or after, but only the *wholeness* of the enduring sacred order.

The astonishing, auto-idolatrous hubris of Freud's view of religion is succinctly expressed in the following passage by Dr. R. R. Greenson, a respected contemporary professor of psychiatry:

> The Devil and God, said Freud, are both derived from the father. God, as he is perceived by children, is an exalted father figure. . . . Satan is created out of the hateful impulses the child feels toward the terrible, wrathful, and punitive father. The father is thus the prototype of both God and the Devil. Religions teach that God created man in his image. Psychoanalysis, on the other hand, teaches that the child created God out of his primitive perceptions of his father and projects his own feelings and impulses onto his ambivalently loved God.[15]

Anathema sit!

Freud correctly perceived in sex something absolutely fundamental to all other human attitudes and feelings, but he did not discern the true reason: it is a holy symbol of union and reconciliation against which sacrilege is perilously easy to commit. The clear lesson of history is that the decay of a civilization is always accompanied by a breakdown in sexual morality and by the decline of religion. Nor do I believe that the coincidence of these phenomena of social deterioration is accidental. The sacraments of the Christian religion translate the participants into the sacred order of eternity by means of the symbols of a time-bound event, namely, the outward and visible occasion of each particular celebration. It is for this reason (and not merely in support of patriarchy, as some misguided reformers would have us believe) that marriage is numbered among the sacraments. The divinely inspired author of the Song of Songs heads the list of those who, throughout the centuries, have understood that *sexuality itself is a symbol of wholeness, of the reconciliation of opposites, of the loving at-one-ment between God and Creation.* In the words of the great contemporary composer Olivier Messaien (a devout Roman Catholic), ". . . the union of true lovers is for them a transformation on the cosmic scale."[16] This insight is also embodied in the image of the Church as the bride of Christ, which is to be taken together with the most ancient description of marriage, "they two shall become one flesh."

The true religious goal of human sexuality can thus be seen not as *satisfaction,* but as *completeness.*[17] Without this goal of completeness, satisfaction pursued as an end-in-itself deteriorates into lust. It is the dualist error in a subtle form: the body is used as an instrument in the service of a self-centered aim. It matters little whether that self-centered aim is the pleasurable release of physical orgasm, the reproductive pride of producing an heir, or the community pride of living "respectably." These are all, in the end, lusts. The problem with sex is that no other phenomenon of human existence can symbolize the vision of the sacramental universe in which all things are harmoniously connected, and at the same time manifest the tragic discontinuities which were inflicted on us and our world through the Fall. No other human activity so lends itself to subtle, as well as obvious, exploitation both of self and of others.

Throughout this book I have described the ways in which men and women differ from one another. I have also reviewed many of the ways in which the consciousness and the fear or resentment of that difference have moved men and women to exploit either themselves or one another, often both at once. I do not believe that it is accidental in the general evolutionary scheme of things that we are now simultaneously emerging from the patriarchial era and realizing that the human family cannot continue to expand indefinitely. If we examine the history of human culture, it becomes evident that the creative possibilities of the uniting of the opposites of the masculine and feminine principles have never been widely understood or implemented up to now except at the biological level. Here men and women unite, and the third, or child, that arises out of their union shares the nature of both. But at the level of consciousness we have always, except in individual blessed matings, been in a different situation. Men and women have not united as equal opposites. They have used one another in different ways, so that real psychological union has seldom occurred. We are clearly moving out of this era; people are no longer satisfied with the old system. This is the silver lining, I believe, to the rising divorce rate. Many people are yearning for a truer, richer union, of mind, heart and spirit, not only that of body and social convenience. The third which will arise from such unions will no longer be only a human child, however desired and welcome such a child may be under appropriate circumstances, but a new consciousness, a new spirit, a new approach to the sacred order. The end, in short, of the perennial "battle of the sexes." In describing the sacred order, I have said that *no* human activity may stand outside of it with impunity, and that therefore *all* human activity must ultimately be religious, whether conceptualized in any conventionally theological language or not. In her brilliant book, *The Feminine,* Ann Ulanov, a professor of Psychiatry and Religion at Union Theological Seminary, has written:

> The feminine . . . is a factor which must be recognized as essential for the full exercise of the religious function. Thus, if the feminine is neglected, undervalued, or misconstrued, the result psychologically is a diminishing of one's growth toward wholeness, and the result theologically is that the *imago dei* does not achieve its full stature.[18]

We have forgotten for too long that this image of God, in which the sacred myth tells us that humanity was created, includes both man and woman. As we try to move toward a less exploitative, more conscious, more responsible understanding of sexuality, we must keep that fact in the forefront of our deliberations. In Chapters Five and Seven I outlined the ways in which homosexuality constitutes a rejection, either partial or total, of the possibility of union with the other sex. Very clearly, the wholeness of the sacred order is neither symbolized nor approximated by sexual practices which are thus grounded in the denial of half of the image of God. Some measure of physical or partial emotional *satisfaction* may be achieved, but the Christian goal of *completeness* is not. John Dixon describes the failure of homosexuality in these words:

> It is not a valid mode or model of sexuality for it affirms the incompleteness. I cannot affirm my wholeness except in the other who is truly other. It is probably true that any love is better than no love in a loveless world. But love is not a single, lone act isolated from other acts. It is part of a whole, the ordering of relation. It communicates a sense of the structure, of the forming of paradigms. . . . Fulfillment must be found outside the self if it is to affect the self. But in sexual matters fulfillment is completeness, the coming together of differences.[19]

In the recent Vatican statement, *Declaration on Certain Questions Concerning Sexual Ethics,* which reiterated the Church's traditional position with regard to the "disordered" quality of all sexual acts outside of marriage, homosexuality was condemned in these words: "For according to the objective moral order [natural law], homosexual relations are acts which lack an essential and indispensable finality."[20] The finality which is meant is that of the possibility of procreation as an essential ingredient of a morally acceptable sexual act. This formulation fails to engage the question of the *symbolic* significance of the sexual act, which is what gives it its sacramental character. I do not believe that it is any longer possible, in the present state of the world's history, to defend the once appropriate idea that the mysteries of sexuality are all contained in the physical act of procreation. On the contrary, I believe that procreation itself is a symbol of still deeper rich mysteries which we are only beginning to glimpse.

As Christians we must eschew selfish and hedonistic goals, not only for sexuality but for everything else as well. The serious Christian examination of what these goals may be has only just begun. If we accept the view of sexuality as symbolic, and I think the evidence for that is incontrovertible, then it is no doubt true that we will never exhaust the meanings, no matter how long we may continue to consider them. By its very nature, a living symbol is a bottomless well. But I have no doubt that Dixon's formulation of the mystery of completeness to be achieved only by encountering the *truly other* will stand as among the most important, the richest, and most enduring of those meanings.

Homosexuality is, in the end, a symbolic confusion.

Appendix A
On Ordination of Homosexuals to the Priesthood

I conclude that homosexuality is not a normal alternate lifestyle, but a failure in human adaptation. This failure may range from forms which by any standards would be considered abnormal and perverse, to forms which constitute an isolated pocket of immaturity. However, at best it is an immaturity, and immaturity is morally significant.

Homosexual practice does not lead toward the true goals of human sexuality. In some cases it may not lead the participants any further away from these goals than they are already, and perhaps may serve other goals which are necessary for the person concerned. But these cannot partake of the sacramental character which human sexuality is intended to have.

What are the implications of this book for the question of ordination? Should a person's sexual orientation be a factor in considering suitability for the priesthood?

1) No homosexual should be ordained who believes and proclaims that homosexuality is normal and entirely acceptable.

2) Since perfection is hardly a standard for priesthood, homosexuality cannot be in and of itself disqualifying. Persons with other known and confessed immaturities have been and will continue to be ordained.

3) *Thorough* spiritual and psychiatric examination of *all* candidates for the priesthood should be carried out. These examinations must include investigation of sexuality, since that is an important factor in psychological and spiritual development. Any candidate who is subsequently discovered to have lied about this or any other aspect of the examination should be automatically disqualified.

The particular configuration of sexual adaptation in candidates with that condition should be carefully examined to avoid accepting those persons whose serious immaturities are not appropriately confined. In addition, it should be recognized that there are some types of ministry which would present special difficulties for some homosexuals. These possibilities should be particularly noted in order to avoid placements which might be inordinately problematic. For example, some types of suburban parishes might subject the male priest to nearly continuous exposure to women, many of whom would place very heavy demands on the rector in the form of excessive need for counseling, support, arbitration of differences of opinion, and, not infrequently, outright seductiveness. This degree of exposure to these sorts of women would far exceed that which would ordinarily be encountered in other occupations or in other clerical placements. Some configurations of the homosexual adaptation would be unduly stressed by such situations, which could result in unnecessary psychological decompensation or in acting out the homosexuality in some impulsive way, even though such behavior might not be characteristic under more normal conditions.

4) There will be differences of opinion as to whether it would ever be appropriate to allow homosexual priests to preside over the young as their principal role. It could be argued that, precisely to the extent that the priest was an admirable person and a good role model in other respects, vulnerable young people might become confused, even if the priest were earnestly urging them to continue the growth process toward heterosexual adaptation. At the same time, there have been many homosexual priests who have been very gifted in working with young people and who have found in such work a satisfying and rewarding outlet for their otherwise thwarted parental talents. The decision in individual cases should be made carefully according to whatever special circumstances might exist. I believe it would probably be unwise to assign to youth work a priest whose homosexual orientation was publicly acknowledged. This culture, however, is altogether too curious and interfering about the sexual inclinations and habits of single people.

Appendix B
On the Interpretation of Biblical Texts Referring to Homosexuality

There can be no reasonable doubt that the Bible, in numerous places in both the Old and New Testaments, specifically forbids homosexual acts, referring to them as unclean, an abomination, and in other negative terms. In order to decide how we should look at these texts, it is important to recall the distinction drawn in Chapter Twelve between *principles* and *rules.* Many other things are also forbidden in scripture which few people would now find necessary to take literally (such as women covering their heads in church). Still other customs are tolerated in scripture (such as slavery) which we no longer feel are appropriate expressions of the underlying principles of religion.

Sometimes the decision to abandon a rule has clearly followed an apparently inevitable secular development. An interesting example of this was the controversy over lending money at interest, a practice specifically forbidden in both Old and New Testaments. The debate over this question raged for more than five centuries and was not settled until the eighteenth century, after much hair-splitting finally drew a distinction between usury (exorbitant) and interest (reasonable). At other times, the reinterpretation of rules has had more of a prophetic character; those who are conscientious objectors in time of war illustrate this mode, as do many of those who oppose the death penalty.

At the present very few theologians are strict biblical literalists. They attempt, rather, to discern the underlying meaning, the governing principles, the enduring message of the sacred writings. This is as it should be. Therefore, those who oppose homosexuality cannot rest their case on mere quotation of the texts which forbid it. They must also appeal (as I have tried to do in Part

IV) to the underlying principles which the texts exemplify, as well as to the general message of religion taken as a whole.

Precisely because literalism is not an appropriate theological mode of scriptural interpretation, I find unacceptable those pro-homosexual arguments which attempt to deny the clear statements of the texts. These appear to be an illogical attempt to have it both ways: on the one hand, one does not have to take texts literally, but on the other hand, one can still appeal to those same texts if one can only show that they say something else! In particular, I object to the revisionist interpretation of the Sodom and Gomorrah myth which claims that inhospitality to strangers rather than homosexuality was the offense in question. It is alleged that the Hebrew word *yādhá* used in Genesis 19:5, usually translated "know" in English, does not refer to sexual relations in this instance. I have questioned several Hebrew scholars about this, all of whom have given the opinion that in this passage, as well as in most others (including Genesis 4:1 where "Adam 'knew' his wife Eve, and she conceived . . ."), the meaning is clearly sexual. To suppose otherwise is to make nonsense of the rest of the story; if the men of Sodom had no sexual intentions toward Lot's visitors, why would Lot have replied "I beg you, my brothers, do no such wicked thing. Listen, I have two daughters who are virgins. I am ready to send them out to you, to treat as it pleases you. But as for the men, do nothing to them, for they have come under the shadow of my roof" (Genesis 19:7–9). At the same time, there is no reason to imagine that homosexual practices were the only, or even the principal sin which led God to destroy the cities. Many different kinds of wickedness are ascribed to Sodom and Gomorrah in references to the event throughout the rest of the Bible. The simplest appeal to ordinary human experience would suggest that people capable of the kind of violent, dehumanized, exploitative behavior described in the above passage are hardly likely to have been model citizens in other respects. My own opinion, therefore, is that they were singled out for destruction because of total, irredeemable wickedness of all kinds. In fact, if there were no other scriptural references to homosexuality, one could certainly not use this story in objection to it, any more than one could use a story about rape to support a condemnation of heterosexuality.

The other texts, however, are not equivocal in this way. Their interpretation, like that of all texts referring to all kinds of sexual behavior, requires a coherent view of biblical *principles* governing sexual relations, as well as an understanding of the significance, symbolic and otherwise, of sexuality in general. As described in Part IV, my view is that homosexuality is not consonant with these principles. At the same time, it must be noted that our understanding of the *principles* of compassion and forgiveness must lead us to change the *rules* laid out in scripture for the punishment of sexual offenses. To accept the biblical model of monogamous, lifelong, heterosexual marriage as the *ideal* (from which all other behavior is at best a sad if humanly inevitable departure, and at worst is exploitative lust) is by no means to justify, condone, or excuse in any way the cruel and unusual punishments which have been meted out to sexual offenders of all kinds in the past.

Notes

Chapter 1

1. Bertrand Russell, *Autobiography of Bertrand Russell* (Boston: Atlantic, Little, Brown, 1968), p. 100; quotation from letter to Constance Malleson, October 23, 1916.

2. C. S. Lewis, *The Problem of Pain* (New York: Macmillan Paperbacks, 1962), p. 21.

3. C. G. Jung, *The Undiscovered Self* (Boston: Little, Brown, 1957), *passim.*

4. Rosemary Haughton, *The Theology of Experience* (New York: Newman Press, 1972).

Chapter 2

1. Arno Karlen, *Sexuality and Homosexuality* (New York: W. W. Norton & Co., 1971), p. 5.

2. Karlen, *op. cit.,* p. 34.

3. Alfred Leslie Rowse, *The Elizabethan Renaissance: The Life of the Society* (New York: Scribner's, 1971) pp. 187–88.

4. George Domino, "Homosexuality and Creativity," *Sandoz Psychiatric Spectator*, March 1974.

5. Laurie Schneider, "Donatello's Bronze David," *The Art Bulletin* 55 (June 1973).

6. John W. Dixon, Jr., "The Drama of Donatello's David," paper presented at the American Academy of Religion, November 1, 1975. In press.

7. Francis King, *Sexuality, Magic and Perversion* (Secaucus, New Jersey: The Citadel Press, 1974). In pp. 108–14 are the records of a homosexual ritual performed by the notorious black magician, Aleister Crowley, who died in

1947. Chapter 12, pp. 122–41, attempts to refute the charge that systematic homosexual magical rites were ever common in occultism—but this is done in the course of describing at least one instance of just that. The author denies the charges of Dion Fortune (pen name of Mrs. Violet Firth Evans), founder of the Society of the Inner Light, a Christian esoteric order active in England to the present day; she claimed throughout her writings that this practice was, if not common, at least frequent enough to be of concern. My own researches into the occult movements presently flourishing in New England have turned up two such instances in the last three years. Reliable informants in both England and in Switzerland report similar cults in those countries. The practice of heterosexual magical rituals is still more common. The obvious, well publicized instance is the "Manson Family."

Dion Fortune (Violet Firth-Evans), *Sane Occultism* (London: The Aquarian Press, 1967), pp. 125–46.

8. Karlen, *op. cit.;* p. 483. (Italics mine.)

Chapter 3

1. Karlen, *op. cit.,* p. 399. Transcript of a taped interview with Dr. Frank Beach.

2. C. A. Tripp, *The Homosexual Matrix* (New York: McGraw-Hill Book Co., 1975).

Chapter 4

1. *Diagnostic and Statistical Manual of Mental Disorders II* (Washington, D.C.: American Psychiatric Association, 1968), p. 44.

2. *Ibid.,* p. 44. A more detailed description of the circumstances surrounding the nomenclature change, along with bibliographical references to the technical literature, can be found in Charles W. Socarides' "Homosexuality is Not Just an Alternate Life Style" in *Male and Female,* Ruth Tiffany Barnhouse and Urban T. Holmes, III, eds. (New York: The Seabury Press, 1976), pp. 145–56.

Chapter 5

1. Irving Bieber et. al., *Homosexuality* (New York: Random House, 1962).

2. Karlen, *op. cit.,* p. 572–73.

3. Karlen, *op. cit.,* p. 574, quotation from Bieber.

4. Lawrence J. Hatterer, *Changing Homosexuality in the Male* (New York: McGraw-Hill Book Co., 1970), p. 2. The title of this book is slightly mislead-

ing, since it does not refer merely to those cases where change to heterosexuality is meant. Dr. Hatterer is describing not only that, but also whatever level or form of change may be possible in a particular case, from troubled and unstable homosexual life styles toward forms of that adaptation which can provide better adjustment and security than the patient had initially.

5. Karlen, *op. cit.*, p. 579.

6. Tripp, *op. cit.*, pp. 57–58.

7. Tripp, *op. cit.*, p. 64.

8. Tripp, *op. cit.*, p. 65.

9. Tripp, *op. cit.*, p. 48.

10. Tripp, *op. cit.*, p. 62.

11. Tripp, *op. cit.*, p. 80.

12. Tripp, *op. cit.*, p. 82.

13. Tripp, *op. cit.*, p. 35.

14. Tripp, *op. cit.*, p. 259.

15. Karlen, *op.cit.*, pp. 521–23.

16. Adrian Sondheimer, "Teen Claim of Homosexuality Held Assertion of Independence" in *Clinical Psychiatry News,* Vol. 4, no. 5 (May 1976).

Chapter 6

1. The following four books, arranged in order from the simplest to the most complex exposition, will provide a good understanding of Jung's view of the feminine principle and its interrelations with the masculine principle. Irene Claremont de Castillejo, *Knowing Woman* (New York: Putnam & Sons, 1973).

Emma Jung, *Animus and Anima* (New York: Spring Publications, 1972).

Esther M. Harding, *Woman's Mysteries* (New York: Bantam Books, 1973).

Ann Belford Ulanov, *The Feminine in Jungian Psychology and Christian Theology* (Evanston, Ill.: Northwestern University Press, 1971).

2. C. G. Jung, "Answer to Job," *Collected Works of C. G. Jung,* Bollingen Series XX, Vol. 11 (Princeton: Princeton University Press, 1969), p. 395, par. 620.

3. Alex Comfort, *The Joy of Sex* (New York: Crown Publishers, 1972), *passim.*

4. Irving Singer, *The Goals of Human Sexuality* (New York: W. W. Norton & Co., Inc., 1973), p. 14 ff.

5. "The *Redbook* Report: A Study of Female Sexuality" (New York: *Redbook* Magazine, June, September and October, 1975 issues).

6. Natalie Shainess, "How 'Sex Experts' Debase Sex," *World Magazine* (January 2, 1973), pp. 21–25.

Judd Marmor, "In Defense of Masters and Johnson," *World Magazine* (January 30, 1973), pp. 24–27.

7. Kenneth Kenniston, "The Physiological Fallacy," *Contemporary Psychology*, 3/67, p. 113–15. About Masters and Johnson's work he says: ". . . a treatise whose objectivity is flawed by physiological reductionism, methodological naivete, and ethical insensitivity." ". . . what they term 'psychologic factors' invariably turn out to be reports of sexual sensations, that is, the subjective awareness of physiology."

8. Tripp, *op. cit.,* p. 19.

9. Tripp, *op. cit.,* p. 21.

Chapter 7

1. This quotation is from the foreword I wrote to a fine little book which I recommend very highly. The author is a Jungian analyst who describes the vicissitudes of the male maturation process as well as adult problems with the *anima*—all in terms of an exposition of the symbolism of the Parsifal legend.

Robert Johnson, "He!" (King of Prussia, Pa.: Religious Publishing House, 1974).

2. Betty Friedan, *The Feminine Mystique* (New York: W. W. Norton & Co., Inc., 1963), see especially Chapter 9, "The Sexual Sell."

3. Wilson Bryan Key, *Subliminal Seduction* (Englewood Cliffs, N. J.: Prentice-Hall, 1973). This well documented book exposes, in terrifying and disgusting detail, the lengths to which subliminal stimulation of unconscious primitive fears and instincts has been carried for purely commercial motives. Those who didn't believe in the Devil will find him alive and well and living on Madison Avenue.

4. Margaret Adams, *Single Blessedness* (New York: Basic Books, 1976). Most highly recommended, a valuable antidote to the view that marriage is the only appropriate lifestyle; written by a witty, literate woman who is neither homosexual nor a man-hater.

5. Signe Hammer, *Daughters and Mothers, Mothers and Daughters* (New York: Quadrangle/The New York Times Book Co., 1975), pp. xv–xvi.

6. Ruth-Jean Eisenbud, "Female Homosexuality, A Sweet Enfranchisement" in *Modern Woman, Her Psychology and Sexuality,* George D. Goldman and Donald S. Milman, eds. (Springfield: Charles C. Thomas, 1969).

Chapter 8

1. Evelyn Hooker, "Male Homosexuality in the Rorschach," *Journal of Projective Techniques,* 22 (1958), pp. 33–54.

2. Samuel Hadden, "Homosexuality: Its Questioned Classification," *Psychiatric Annals* (April 1976), vol. 6, no. 4, pp. 38–46.

3. This paragraph is taken from my article, "On Being a Christian Psychiatrist," *New Life* (March 1974).

4. Hatterer, *op. cit.,* p. 86.

5. Tripp, *op. cit.,* p. 245.

6. Tripp, *op. cit.,* p. 250.

7. Alfred Kinsey, Wardell B. Pomeroy, Clyde E. Martin, *Sexual Behavior in the Human Male* (Philadelphia: W. B. Saunders Co., 1948), p. 658.

8. Unfortunately, there are many books on the market today which draw on professional literature in a way which will probably deceive most laypeople, but which betray to the trained expert an appalling ignorance. A particularly unfortunate example—precisely because the issue is so important in the contemporary church and a good, reliable book on the subject was therefore badly needed—is the recent book by Donald Goergen, *The Sexual Celibate* (New York: The Seabury Press, 1975).

9. Karlen, *op. cit.,* interview with Dr. Konietzko, p. 569.

Chapter 9

1. Robert Stroller, "Overview: The Impact of New Advances in Sex Research on Psychoanalytic Theory," *American Journal of Psychiatry* 130 (March 1973), p. 246.

2. Stoller, *op. cit.,* p. 247.

3. Stoller, *op. cit.,* 249. (Italics mine.)

4. Edrita Fried, *The Ego in Love and Sexuality* (New York: Grune & Stratton, 1960), p. 32.

5. Irving Kristol, "Discipline as a Dirty Word," *Saturday Review World* (June 1, 1974).

6. Alan Jones, "Male and Female Created He Them," *Anglican Theological Review* 57 (October 1975), p. 441.

7. Samuel Taylor Coleridge, "Kubla Khan" in *The Portable Coleridge,* I. A. Richards, ed. (New York: Viking Press, 1950), p. 157.

8. Robert Capon, *Supper of the Lamb* (New York: Doubleday, 1969).

9. Norman Pittenger, "A Theological Approach to Understanding Homosexuality" in *Male and Female: Christian Approaches to Sexuality,* Ruth Tiffany Barnhouse and Urban T. Holmes, III, eds. (New York: The Seabury Press, 1976).

William Muehl's "Some Words of Caution" in *Male and Female* should also be read; it exposes the dangers and fallacies in the premise that all expressions of love are self-justifying.

Chapter 10

1. Mrs. Emma F. Angell Drake, M. D., *What Every Young Wife Ought to Know* (Philadelphia: Vir Publishing Co., 1908), p. 87.
2. Drake, *op. cit.,* p. 89.
3. J. M. Cameron, "Sex In The Head," *New York Review of Books* (May 13, 1976), pp. 19–28. (If you have old copies of this periodical stacked up somewhere, by all means take the trouble to dig out this issue! If not, the article is more than worth a special trip to the library.)
4. Cameron, *op. cit.*

Chapter 11

1. Genesis 2 and 3 contain the full account. *Jerusalem Bible.*
2. Alan Westin, *Privacy and Freedom* (New York: Atheneum, 1967), p. 36.
3. *The Book of Common Prayer* (New York: Church Pension Fund, 1928), p. 17.
4. Karl Menninger, *What Ever Became of Sin?* (New York: Hawthorn Books, 1973), *passim.*
5. John J. McNeill, S. J., *The Church and the Homosexual* (Kansas City: Sheed Andrews and McMeel, Inc., 1976), p. 184.

Chapter 12

1. McNeill, *op. cit.,* p. 193.
2. McNeill, *op. cit.,* p. 194.
3. McNeill, *op. cit.,* p. 194.
4. Lynn Turgeon, "Notes on the New China," *The Center Magazine,* Vol. V., No. 6, (Nov.-Dec. 1972), p. 58.
5. Turgeon, *op. cit.,* p. 52.
6. Richard Wilhelm and Cary F. Baynes (trans.), *The I Ching or Book of Changes,* Bollingen Series XIX, 3rd ed. (Princeton: Princeton University Press, 1967), p. 123.
7. McNeill, *op. cit.,* p. 196.
8. C. G. Jung, "Psychotherapy Today," *Collected Works of C. G. Jung,* Bollingen Series XX, Vol. 16 (Princeton: Princeton University Press, 1941).
9. McNeill, *op. cit.,* p. 198. (Emphasis added.)
10. Cameron, *op. cit.* (Emphasis added.)
11. Rosemary Haughton, *op. cit.*
12. Romans 2:29.
13. Charles Davis, *Body as Spirit: The Nature of Religious Feeling* (New

York: The Seabury Press, 1976). This excellent book by a former Roman Catholic theologian explores this topic in some detail. It is particularly valuable for its distinction between *sensuousness,* which is perceived as expressing appropriately the body/spirit unity, and *sensuality,* which is the use of the body for its own dissociated aims. The old word *lust* comes to mind. The essential participation of body and feeling for full religious realization is underscored.

14. Anthony C. Storr, *C. G. Jung* (New York: Viking Press, 1973), p. 13.

15. R. R. Greenson, "A Psychoanalyst's Indictment of *The Exorcist,*" *Saturday Review World* (June 15, 1974).

16. Olivier Messaien, "Turangalila Symphony," notes by the composer on record jacket (New York: RCA LSC-7051, 1968).

17. John W. Dixon, Jr., "The Sacramentality of Sex" in *Male and Female,* Ruth Tiffany Barnhouse and Urban T. Holmes, III, eds. (New York: The Seabury Press, 1976). This article really should be read in its entirety in order to appreciate the wonderfully revealing sublety of Dixon's argument.

18. Ulanov, *op. cit.,* p. 146.

19. Dixon, *op. cit.*

20. "Declaration on Certain Questions Concerning Sexual Ethics" (Washington, D.C.: Sacred Congregation for the Doctrine of the Faith, United States Catholic Conference, December 29, 1975), pp. 8 and 9 especially.

Index